Insight Out

Peter Marks was born in Melbourne in 1955, and is immensely over-qualified to be of any use to anybody. He has degrees in Economics and Law, and an MBA from Edinburgh University. Over the past twelve years Peter has worked in many facets of finance including merchant banking in London and Melbourne as well as in stockbroking. He currently holds a senior position within the securities industry. Peter's interests include cycling, travel, classical music (he plays the french horn, at a professional level), and honing his life skills. He is married, has three children and lives in Melbourne.

Peter Schmideg was born in an unpronounceable town in Hungary in 1954, arriving in Melbourne at the age of two as a refugee, fleeing from the Hungarian Revolution (no, it's not a restaurant). Peter has a degree in Art History, and has been working as a copywriter in the advertising industry since 1977. He has been successfully running his own business since 1981, including a few years based in London. Peter's interests include, apart from the never-ending refinement of life skills, regular cycling, reading and attempting to learn piano. He is married, has two children and lives in Melbourne.

Insight Out

Life's great possibilities

Peter Marks & Peter Schmideg

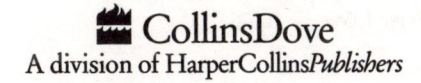

CollinsDove
A division of HarperCollins*Publishers*

To my parents Eva and Stan, to all my family
and to the memory of Robert, an inspiration to us all
P.M.

To the memory of my parents Manci and Zoli
and to my wonderful family
P.S.

Published by Collins Dove
A division of HarperCollins*Publishers* (Australia) Pty Ltd
22–24 Joseph Street
North Blackburn Victoria 3130 Australia

© Copyright Peter Marks and Peter Schmideg 1995
All rights reserved. Except as provided by Australian copyright law, no part of this book may be reproduced without permission in writing from the publishers.

First published 1995
Designed by Pier Vido
Cover design by Pier Vido
Typeset by Collins Dove Typesetting
Printed in Australia by McPherson's Printing Group

The National Library of Australia
Cataloguing-in-Publication Data:

Marks, Peter, 1955–
   Insight out.

   ISBN 1 86371 304 2.

   1. Life skills. 2. Self-management (Psychology).
   I. Schmideg, Peter, 1954–   . II. Title.

158.1

Contents

About the authors   *i*
Introduction   *xi*

Part one
Attitudes, beliefs and values

1. Who are you?   *3*
2. The journey: looking back, looking forward   *7*
3. Self-image and self-talk—listening to your inner voices   *11*
4. Personal baggage: will you get charged excess?   *15*
5. Living up or down to expectations   *18*
6. Taking responsibility for choices   *21*
7. De-compartmentalise your life—removing the boxes we live in   *24*
8. Trust and honesty: trick or treat?   *28*
9. What are you worth?   *32*
10. Being competitive: who wins, who loses?   *35*
11. When is a problem an opportunity?   *40*
12. Positive thinking: friend or foe?   *44*

Part two
Emotions and feelings

13. Feeling, recognising and dealing with emotions   *51*
14. Denial, anger and guilt   *55*
15. Respect and esteem: the face in the mirror   *59*
16. Love and other desires: being connected to ourselves and others   *63*
17. Levels of consciousness   *67*
18. Our emotional choices—dealing with life's dilemmas   *71*
19. Insight, wisdom and courage   *74*

Part three
Learning, thinking and planning

20 Planning your life: developing your personal mission statement *81*
21 Structure, strategy, goals—which comes first? *85*
22 Mentor worship: from hero to zero *88*
23 Knowledge, intelligence and wisdom *92*
24 Perceptions and reality—what is the difference? *95*
25 Learning from our experiences—breaking familiar patterns; establishing new ones *99*
26 Priorities and focus—the secret ingredients *104*
27 Discipline, determination and persistence (DDP) *107*
28 Attention to detail—nothing works without it *112*
29 Procrastination—I'll tell you what it means tomorrow *116*
30 The problems of problem-solving *120*
31 Does your 'dream gauge' show 'full' or 'empty'? *125*
32 The patience perspective *128*
33 It's about time *134*

Part four
Relating and communicating

34 Relating and relationships—putting in and taking out *141*
35 Dealing with people: it takes all types *144*
36 Changing others or yourself—which comes first? *148*
37 Comparing yourself to others—the big trap *151*
38 Peer groups—can you handle the pressure? *155*
39 Talking straight: say what you mean, mean what you say *158*
40 Listening and understanding *161*
41 Negotiation and conflict resolution *164*
42 Beware the hidden agenda *168*
43 Body language: the hidden clues *171*
44 Inner space, outer space *175*

Part five
Living and working

45	Recognising strengths: accepting and dealing with weaknesses	*181*
46	Planned vs unplanned careers: keeping your options open	*185*
47	Opportunity knocks	*189*
48	A job: career path or dead end?	*192*
49	Climbing the ladder—just watch the grease	*198*
50	Standing still or moving on—the mission statement check-up	*201*
51	Job security: the myth	*204*
52	Losing your job and other setbacks: opportunity knocks again	*208*
53	Creating a balance: work to live or live to work	*212*
54	Mind and body: keeping both fit	*217*
55	Humour and other escape valves	*220*
56	The power of creativity and imagination	*223*

Part six
Financial security or insecurity

57	Money: handle with care	*229*
58	Status and wealth	*234*
59	Needs and wants: what's the difference?	*237*
60	Spend now or spend later?	*241*
61	Savings: a regular habit	*244*
62	Financial planning and budgeting: does it work?	*247*

Part seven
Change and empowerment

63	Taking control of your life—the choices are yours	*253*
64	The Near Life Experience	*257*
65	The fear of failure	*260*
66	Stress	*263*
67	Developing a higher purpose: a view from the top	*267*
68	Empowering others—what it's all about	*270*

Part eight
Insight out

69	The best things in life are free	*275*
70	Stop and smell the roses	*278*
71	Is everything okay?	*280*
72	Your life as an adventure	*282*
73	Being present: enjoy the 'now'	*285*

Further reading *289*

Acknowledgements

There are very few books that aren't collaborative efforts, and this is no exception. Many friends, family members and associates contributed either knowingly or unknowingly to the book in both structure and content.

Over twenty years ago our eyes were opened to our personal potential as a result of many fascinating conversations with a fellow student and friend by the name of James Milojkovic. He remains a friend and to this day is still helping people realise their full potential.

We would also like to thank all at Collins Dove for their support and encouragement throughout the lengthy writing and editing process. Thank you to Robin Freeman and our editor Anne Boyd, who believed in the project from the first moment. Anne's comments and guidance have been invaluable. We would also like to thank Maggie Richardson who, with her faithful Macintosh, typed and re-typed our manuscript and was available at all sorts of strange hours for last minute changes and additions.

Thanks must also go to our respective parents who provided us with the basic raw materials, skills and determination to embark on this project.

Peter Marks would like to make special mention of Dr Sara Murphy for being a key witness and guide throughout this journey and pointing out many important signs along the way.

We would also like to thank our wives Lee Ann (PM) and Deborah (PS) who allowed us the indulgence of writing every spare moment we had between work and family commitments including evenings and weekends. We appreciate your love, support and patience during the entire development and writing process.

Finally, thank you to those too numerous to mention who have in one way or another left an indelible mark on our lives; and in saying this, we also acknowledge the ongoing contribution which we have made to each other's lives during a friendship spanning twenty-three years.

Peter Marks and Peter Schmideg
Melbourne, September 1994

Introduction

Have you ever taken a long hard look at yourself and tried to determine what sort of person you really are? What are your priorities? What drives you? Have you ever been perplexed by your behaviour, your motives, your feelings? Have you ever thought about your inner and outer self, the public and private aspects of your personality?

This book is about integrating the various facets of ourselves so that we can lead an authentic, harmonious and enriching life. A glance through the contents pages will show how wide-ranging the topics are, topics that are all inextricably linked to each other. Some of the information will be challenging, if not confronting, but without facing certain realities how else will you grow and change?

How did we come to write this book? For the past twenty years we have been preoccupied with the idea of gaining greater control over our own lives. Twenty years ago we were university students exploring how to take control, and embrace all life has to offer. In our own amateur, but inquisitive, way we explored a whole range of subjects, including motivation, behaviour, attitudes, beliefs, popular psychology, personal development. We mixed with that a healthy dose of Eastern philosophies such as Zen and the *Tao Te Ching*. When other people our age were seemingly preoccupied with discussing the latest nightspot, or which alloy wheel to buy for their car, we were discussing our motives for doing things. We were looking at others and just asking 'why?' all the time. With another friend, we even formed an informal club, a not-too-serious forum for discussing anything from behaviour to ego to status symbols and competitiveness—anything that would help our

INTRODUCTION

understanding of how people tick and why they behave the way they do.

Then, as today, we were interested in understanding the underlying causes of behaviour, as well as the ramifications of that behaviour. In other words, if we were to continue along a certain path, with a particular attitude or mind-set, how would that affect us later on? How would that shape our outlook, and how would others perceive us? We truly believe that all aspects of our lives are linked, so that what happens in one area of life has a profound impact in other areas. We believe we are responsible for our own actions, choices and lives. We need to look at our lives as a whole and make choices based on becoming an integrated person.

Over the years, our interests in this area have deepened, as we practised our own life skills. We have never 'grown out' of looking at life issues, as some suggested (and hoped) we might. The sifting and filtering process has, over a considerable period, led to the creation of this handbook of ideas, thoughts, accumulated knowledge and, hopefully, some insight. The book is about trying to understand the stuff we are made of, and why we are such a complex bundle of feelings, beliefs, ideas and so on.

This book includes information that you would like to know now, but might not otherwise learn until you're much older. It contains ideas that you can think about and apply in your daily life. We should make it clear at the outset that this isn't the usual motivational or self-help book. It is more a map for a journey than a description of the destination. Furthermore, the book isn't peppered with quick fixes and slogans. We firmly believe that there are no quick fixes, and that lasting progress, and a real shift in one's life, can only take place by taking a holistic approach, by understanding people as a whole. It is also important to be able to *apply* the

INTRODUCTION

knowledge and insight gained. A lot of books focus on the 'self'. But we live in a world with over four billion other 'selves' and need not only to enrich our own lives, but also to acquire the skills to enrich the lives of others.

While this is the sort of book that we would have loved to have read twenty years ago, it is not just a book for those setting out on life's journey. It is also a book for anyone wishing to enhance their life and create a framework for growth. This is a book to dip into, and return to as a regular source of refreshment and ideas.

This book is about learning and gaining insight—into ourselves and others. It represents the beginning of a never-ending journey.

Part 1

Attitudes, beliefs and values

1 Who are you?

What are we made up of? On a physical level we are flesh and blood, but there's more to a human than what we can see and touch. What are we made up of in an intellectual sense? What makes us 'tick'? Our identity comes from all sorts of nebulous things, such as attitudes, beliefs, values, insights, feelings and emotions. We can add a lot more to that list, such as hopes, fears, dreams, ideas, childhood experiences, genetic make-up and so on, but the initial list is a good starting point. We rarely have any insight as to where these 'mind-sets' come from and what impact they have on our lives. How do these attributes affect our response to external events? How do they shape our thinking? This first section deals with a whole range of attitudes, beliefs and values, which are fundamental to understanding who we are and 'what' we are.

How do we define these terms?

Beliefs: Principles, propositions or ideas accepted as true.

Values: The moral principles and beliefs or accepted standards of a person or social group.

Attitudes: The way a person views something, or behaves towards it—often in an evaluative way.

How do you feel right now? Take a few moments to think about what determines your state of mind. There are physical factors, for example. Are you healthy? Are you cold or hungry? Then there are the more complex emotional factors. Are you happy? Are you sad? Do you feel at peace with yourself, or is there endless chatter in your mind? Are you confident or shy? Do you fear each day, or do you face it with courage and anticipation? Are you willing to take risks, or do you always choose the easy way out? Your attitudes, beliefs and general approach to the world, and your state of mind, have an enormous impact on the person you are right now, as well as the person you would like to be.

The next point to consider is what you want to get out of your life. This is a question that only you can answer. But this answer must take account of state of mind. It must take account of the assumptions you make about yourself, how you interact with other people and how you see your role in the world. If your assumptions are incorrect, or slightly skewed, you could arrive at all sorts of different conclusions. Here are a couple of examples.

Long ago, before Columbus 'discovered' America in 1492, many people assumed that the world was flat. That meant that if you sailed off in any one direction, you would eventually fall off the edge as if over a waterfall and be eaten by dragons, or whatever else inhabited that 'twilight zone' at the edge of the Old World. This assumption, which was very firmly believed, held back exploration, because people lived in fear of what lay beyond the horizon. The incorrect assumption led to some rather strange thinking.

You may be driving a car and assuming you are heading in a particular direction. Everything is okay. You're feeling good; the car's going well, some music is playing on the audio system. There is no reason you shouldn't feel good, after all you're acting on an assumption—no, more than that, you are acting on a belief—that you are heading in the right direction. But what if you are wrong? What if you are,

WHO ARE YOU?

in fact, way off course? Sometimes we keep on travelling in a particular direction without knowing that we are going the wrong way. What is even worse is to continue down a particular path knowing that we are wrong.

These examples illustrate how your state of mind and assumptions could be giving you the wrong signals, and taking you in the wrong direction. You could be making assumptions about yourself, and others, that are totally inaccurate, and that prevent you from achieving your real potential.

So, how do you know if you are heading in the right direction? Are you a security 'junkie', craving or needing security? You may have been in a job for ten years, but is it ten years of growth and challenge, or is it one year, repeated ten times? What is your attitude to people? Are you a good listener? Are you driven by your ego and insecurity to continually have to impress people and show off? Do you always have to win? Do you feel easily threatened? It's not enough to think that everything will eventually work out, or that someone, or something will intervene and turn your life around. You could end up feeling trapped and worthless, or worse, spend the second half of your life regretting all the things you did or didn't do when you were younger.

> Once you begin to understand yourself, so many things can begin to change and open up. You'll start to happen to things, rather than things happening to you.

Is there something that is holding you back, preventing you from facing a challenge? Take a long hard look at the reasons. Do you fear rejection? Are you filling your mind with endless 'what if' scenarios? Perhaps the time has come to face the challenge and ... surprise yourself.

WHO ARE YOU?

Once you are aware of what and how you think, and can remain alert to what holds you back, you can go a long way to improving the situation. Life skills start right here, with an opportunity to examine and challenge the innermost feelings, attitudes, beliefs, values and assumptions. Once you begin to understand yourself, so many things can begin to change and open up. You'll become more open, receptive and perceptive. You'll start to happen to things, rather than things happening to you. You begin to tap into a rich source of courage and insight which can shape the rest of your life.

2
The journey
looking back, looking forward

Have you ever been to a place where something as insignificant as a smell, a sound, or a pattern of colours has taken you back to a distant childhood memory? A gift you may have received, a new item of clothing, a cake that someone baked.

It's wonderful how we can, in an instant, be transported back in time, as easily as changing channels on TV. We now have the 'Present' button pushed, but imagine if we could push the button marked 'Past', and there we are on the screen: we can see our tenth birthday, our first bike, our first day of high school, our first kiss. Imagine then that there is a button marked 'Future'. Do you dare push it? Or are you content just to view the past and take part in the present?

Being able to see where you are going can be helpful, but, of course, it's only guesswork. Having an idea in your mind about your future direction can also help you focus on the present. If you have some sort of map, this can guide your decision-making. If you want to be a professional sportsperson for example, what you do right now is crucial to the achievement of that eventual goal. If you want to be a film director, decisions you make now about courses and so on will impact on that goal. The future is in your hands.

There is no denying that we are products of our past.

THE JOURNEY

Factors that come into play include a whole range of things such as the characteristics that are determined by our genes, and the environment in which we grew up. Are you a product of a happy family, or a broken home? Did you shift around a lot when you were young? All these factors and more, combine to make us who we are today. But this does not mean that we are prisoners of our past. Our past shouldn't be used as an excuse to refuse to move forward in life. Many world leaders, for example, have emerged from humble, even poor, beginnings. Early wealth and privilege is no guarantee of contentment or success in later life. People often tend to use the past as an excuse for not doing well. You'll hear them say 'My parents never had much, they just worked and worked, so why should my life be any different?' If you have had a sad or unfortunate past, whether you break free or not is largely up to you. That was then, but this is now. There is little point in blaming or denying your past. Accept it, own it, but just understand that your past isn't necessarily a life sentence. Your past does not have to be a prison that holds you captive. You have the ability within you to participate in the creation of your own future.

Let's take another look at our inner TV monitor. We notice that there are actually two 'Future' channel buttons, Future 1 and Future 2. The former shows you doing well at your chosen career. You look happy, unstressed and in control of your destiny. We switch to Future 2. There's someone who doesn't look too happy. He's doing a job he doesn't like and he looks miserable. His whole appearance and body

> ✵
> You are a worthwhile, unique human being. There is no-one else like you anywhere in the world. You can take control right now and decide the future you want.

language tells us that this person is on the losing end. But wait a minute, the face is familiar. It's you! After you get over the shock a thought dawns on you. You have a choice about your future. Of course, it's never as easy as pushing a button, but the choice is yours. If you feel that you are a victim, and that the whole world is against you, that everything you do is wrong, then you can try to turn things around by examining your underlying attitudes, values, and beliefs. You are a worthwhile, unique human being. There is no-one else like you anywhere in the world. You can take control right now and decide the future you want. Once this decision has been made, you begin to build a bridge to your future.

Of course, the degree of control is not limitless. You need to take into consideration your personal circumstances. It's not so much a case of cutting off your ties with the past or even starting again. It could be a matter of doing better what you do, or seeing what opportunities lie hidden in your current situation. Taking control may simply be a matter of gaining greater insight and perception and embracing your past.

Often we need to be able briefly to live in the past, present and future simultaneously. That is where the child, adolescent and adult images combine. You are what you are today because of your past. Your genes, your family, your education, your friends. The past has shaped you. But the present and your current attitudes and abilities are now shaping your future in many different ways.

You need to put some effort into looking at your future. Ask yourself if the present course you are taking will deliver you to the right destinations. We can learn a lot from babies in this regard. Imagine you are playing with a baby. You have a ball in your hand. The baby sees the ball. You place your hands behind you and drop the ball. The baby has no concept that the ball is behind you. At that age, if the baby can't see something, it doesn't exist. Many of us are still like that. If we can't see or imagine something, then maybe it doesn't exist, or it won't happen. We need to have the insight and imagination to understand that if we do 'x' then the consequence is 'y'. If you want to become a doctor, but you don't do well in your science subjects, the consequences are clear. If you want to be a professional musician but don't practise, then you're unlikely to play in the kind of performances you aspire to.

Nothing comes without our understanding in the present what we want for the future, and applying ourselves to achieve that. The future rapidly becomes the present, and we need to visualise achieving that goal.

Consequences of behaviour and assumptions, as we saw in the previous chapter, can have a huge impact on life. Acknowledge where you've been. Understand where you are right now, and take notice of where you are going. If you keep your head in the sand like an ostrich, hoping that it'll be okay, you may be hoping for a long time. Your life isn't a movie where you'll escape in the final reel to a happy ending.

Take responsibility now for your life and your future. Accept the consequences of your behaviour. It's nobody else's responsibility but your own.

3
Self-image and self-talk
listening to your inner voices

Voices, voices all around us. Where do they come from, what do they say to us? Not only do we have voices speaking to us from the outside but we may also hear our inner voices. What do they all mean? Who do we listen to? If we simply listen and respond to what everyone outside is saying we might end up being caught in the 'image trap', trying to behave according to how others see us.

We can also listen to our inner voices—that seemingly endless chatter inside our heads. The problem with our inner voices is that sometimes there seem to be several, all saying different things, approving, judgemental, kind, harsh and even punishing voices. Even though the voices seem contradictory, they are all part of us. Sometimes they seem so confusing and threatening that we ignore them. Instead, we choose to tune into the external voices. Then it seems easier simply to agree with the outer voices in the hope that others will approve of us. We can end up looking good in the eyes of others, which is fine for our image, but not very

Self-image and self-talk

useful for our sense of self and our need to integrate our inner and outer voices. If we simply keep trying to shut out or deny the existence of our inner voices they will eventually come back louder and more insistent. Our refusal to listen to the inner voices, our continuing to respond only to the outer noise, is likely to lead to a sense of disintegration. We will become an image without any identity.

Ben had been very unhappy with the way he looked. While he wasn't sure whether he was unhappy with his physical appearance or just his image, he was sufficiently depressed to want cosmetic surgery to reshape his face. He thought that his appearance conveyed a negative image and that by changing his appearance, he could change his image and feel better about himself.

One day Ben plucked up the courage to visit a leading plastic surgeon, and went ahead with the operation. Within a few weeks he looked quite different. After several months the inner voices that had already so successfully dented his self-image were returning just as loudly as ever. Slowly Ben realised he was wrong to think he could change himself on the inside by changing his external appearance. He had in fact been unhappy with his external appearance because he had been even more unhappy with his inner 'appearance'.

So what can we do to understand the inner voices that appear to damage rather than help our self-image, the voices that force us so desperately to seek comfort and approval from the outside world? One of the first steps is to recognise the difference between the inner and outer voices and then tune in to the inner voices. Learn not to be scared of them but to embrace them as part of yourself. Even if they sound confronting or challenging you need to recognise

Self-image and self-talk

that there may be parts of you that are like this. Unless you can begin to deal with them you cannot become a whole person. And if you cannot be a whole person, you will not be happy with yourself.

We all have different aspects that we judge as good or bad, light or dark. In embracing our 'wholeness' we need to acknowledge all our aspects. If not, we are bound to end up as less than a whole person. There is little point in thinking that we can rebuild our lives, or improve our situation, by moving to another city or going overseas. We soon discover that we can't run away from ourselves. We are still the same person, only the geography has changed. The French have a saying, 'They change their skies, but not their hearts, who travel far from home.'

However, once we start to listen to the inner voices, to give them space, we might begin to understand our inner selves a little better. The voices may reflect thoughts and feelings from our unconscious self. If we are able in some way to integrate these messages into our conscious lives, it is quite likely that we will be far less concerned about how we appear to the outside world. We will be more interested in listening to our inner voices as a way of becoming an integrated person: our own person. Of course the way we deal with these inner voices, particularly the ones we find so confronting and painful, is critical.

> Once you begin to understand your inner self a little better, you can stop worrying about how you relate to the outer world.

Once you begin this process, other aspects of your external behaviour, such as approval seeking or aggressive behaviour, will begin to lose their significance. The need to look good, keep up appearances or present a certain image will become far less of a priority. This is not to suggest that the process of tuning in to your inner voices is an exercise in self-indulgence. On the contrary, once you begin to understand your inner self a little better, you can stop worrying about how you relate to the outer world. You will strengthen your connections with the outer world by bringing your real self to your work, family and relationships. Indeed, for the first time you may begin to enrich not only your own life but also the lives of others.

4
Personal baggage
will you get charged excess?

Every morning, Ray would wake up and begin his regular litany of complaints: I hate my job, my few friends don't really like me, my kids never do what I ask them to do, I never have enough money to buy the things I want, the world is full of horrible people, terrible problems, and so on and on and on. This ritual had gone on for years. In fact it had recently become considerably worse. His wife had reached the point where she couldn't stand it any longer. His children would mock his ritualistic behaviour—they all thought it was a big joke. Indeed, it would have been if it wasn't so sad and destructive.

Ray thought the world owed him everything, including a better deal, and that if he behaved badly, it wasn't his fault. He believed that he deserved better and that the hardships he had suffered had given him the right to behave in the way he did. He was hostile, angry, non-communicative and generally quite nasty towards others. He couldn't understand why he didn't have many friends. On the surface, he didn't seem to care much about this. He failed to comprehend that changing jobs every twelve months wasn't doing much for his stability or his ability to deal with his underlying problems.

Personal baggage

One day, while driving to work, Ray became increasingly impatient and was involved in a serious car accident. A passenger in another car was injured and taken to hospital. Ray couldn't understand how it happened, how all his pent-up anger and frustration could have led to this event.

A few days later he was thinking about what had happened. He started to realise how, for so long, he had been responding to situations and other people in an aggressive way. His responses reflected all the 'baggage' he was carrying with him. His habit of channelling his anger towards others, and living in the past, had completely overshadowed his behaviour. He was caught in a loop of his own making, impossible to recognise, let alone break out of.

Ray had spent his whole life developing an intricate system, crafting ever more elaborate ways of hiding from his true inner self by continuing to punish and blame himself for previous experiences. Ray couldn't recognise how much the past dominated him. Past experiences and failures had provided the perfect excuse for inaction. If he did do something, he just knew he would fail. Ray's attitude and approach to his life lacked any sort of positive insight.

The accident appeared to change all this. Slowly, Ray began to realise how he had made himself a prisoner of his past. He soon accepted that by examining his past, owning and dealing with it, he could be free. Gradually he came to relish his freedom to move on and travel much lighter.

> Once you choose to let useless baggage go, the benefits can be quite miraculous.

Many of us, like Ray, can take a long time just to recognise the baggage we carry around with us every day. The process of shedding it can be slow and often painful, but it can also be quite liberating. One of the first steps is to understand why we have the baggage, where it came

PERSONAL BAGGAGE

from and what it represents. Then comes the process of deciding what parts of it are still likely to be helpful and what parts are not. Once you choose to let useless baggage go, the benefits can be quite miraculous. This is not to say that baggage always has to have a negative influence. Some baggage can have a positive influence, propelling us towards our goal.

It has taken Ray many years to lighten his load, a process that still has some way to go. He is now determined to travel much lighter, recognising that we all pick up baggage from the strangest places and for the weirdest reasons.

It would of course be so much better if we could sort our baggage earlier and learn to lighten the load as we go. The journey might become more rewarding and the scenery more enjoyable.

5
Living up or down to expectations

How often have you seen your life as not really belonging to you? From an early age an enormous range of demands are placed upon us, and we can feel that we live in the shadow of others' expectations—how they expect us to behave, what they want us to do, what they would like us to become. We are confronted by these issues often without really thinking what we want for ourselves. Yet we must consult our own feelings. What sort of person are we? What would we like to become? What aspirations do we set for ourselves? Unless we try to understand our expectations we may find it difficult to avoid simply following long-established patterns set by others.

For years, Helen believed she wanted to be a doctor (despite the fact that she found much of the study uninteresting and not in any real sense resonating with any of her inner desires or passions). She would go around telling friends that her parents had hoped that when she was older she would become a doctor. At one level she even seemed proud of the prospect of becoming one. It seemed as though her parents' expectations of what it meant to be a doctor, the prestige, status and rewards, had captured her imagination, but not much else.

LIVING UP OR DOWN TO EXPECTATIONS

With little more than a cursory thought, at the end of her schooling Helen went straight into medical school. Six years later she graduated and, still without reflecting on why she wanted to be a doctor, she was one. Although she appreciated the high standing of the medical profession within the community, Helen did not know whether she really wanted to be a doctor or whether it was simply meeting the fantasies and expectations of others that held so much appeal. Following her graduation she entered the profession, but over the ensuing years Helen felt an increasing disquiet about her achievements. She started questioning her basic motives in selecting medicine as her profession.

Eventually she passed up the opportunity to progress further in her profession, because she came to realise that she had not at all been driven by her desire to be a doctor but by a desire to fulfil others' expectations of her and be accepted by them. This realisation made Helen determined to redefine what mattered and establish her own expectations of herself. It wasn't long before she decided to change careers completely.

For years Helen had been fascinated by the theatre and the world of design. Determined to combine these interests, she embarked on a course of study that would lead to her becoming a set designer for a small, innovative theatre company. The choice was far from easy and required tremendous courage, commitment and planning. However, for the first time Helen felt that she had begun really to explore what she wanted to do. Even though her design course was very stimulating it was also demanding. She had to balance her job commitments and continue to support herself. Nevertheless, this change of direction resonated far more comfortably with values and beliefs that she had suppressed. For the first time, Helen began to develop a true sense of integration and balance.

Helen's problem was in trying to live up to others' expectations. There can also be problems with living down to expectations.

LIVING UP OR DOWN TO EXPECTATIONS

For years, Michael had maintained a low opinion of himself. His parents and friends always took the time to remind him how badly he was doing at school, how he always made silly mistakes and how in all probability he would never amount to much in life. Indeed, in listening to all this chatter it was clear that people had very low expectations of Michael. Over the years he had obliged them by living down to their expectations, thus reinforcing Michael's very negative feelings about himself.

Despite all this, Michael had always been fascinated by figures. One day, almost by accident, he read an advertisement regarding a book-keeping course being offered for early school leavers. Michael realised that this was a subject he really did enjoy and that he could make something out of it. Even though he knew others would think the course a complete waste of time, that he would fail or drop out, something in Michael pushed him to enrol. He eventually secured a position that he believed would provide him with enormous scope to expand his skills and experience. More importantly, the entire exercise enabled Michael to examine the ways in which he had been going along with others' low expectations and not considering his own voice.

> As with so much in life, there needs to be a balance.

As with so much in life, there needs to be a balance. We need to learn how to assess other people's expectations of us; how to benefit from their positive expectations, learn from their criticisms, and above all arrive at our own assessment of ourselves and what we truly want to do and become.

6
Taking responsibility for choices

Whether we are aware of it or not, every day of our lives we make choices: about relationships, careers, finances, our future, indeed how we conduct every aspect of our lives. Even when we think we are not choosing (because a particular decision is too hard) we are in fact making a choice to do nothing, or to maintain the status quo.

Our choices are fashioned by an enormous range of variables, not least by our attitudes, beliefs and values. These have, in part, also been shaped by our previous choices, as well as by how we really feel about ourselves.

The paths we choose at any stage of life tell us an enormous amount about who we are, how we arrived at our present position in regard to relationships, careers, financial position or emotional well-being. So much of who we are, and where we stand today, is a result of choices we have made along the way. Understanding, even in part, the reasons behind them can be enormously helpful in changing the way we now make decisions. For example, how does the structure of our life determine our decisions? Does it seemingly 'box us in' and limit us, or do we feel liberated?

There are two further dimensions to the issue of choices.

TAKING RESPONSIBILITY FOR CHOICES

> ✯ Why not evaluate your life on a regular basis? Ask yourself 'How am I doing?', 'Am I heading in the right direction?' If not, why not?

One is examining their consequences. These, as we shall see in a later chapter, represent the 'other half' or symmetry of our choices and have a dramatic impact on our lives. The other aspect is our preparedness to take responsibility for the choices we have made. In taking responsibility, we begin to acknowledge in a real sense our role in determining the direction of our lives. Where we are unhappy with our progress, we can make the necessary changes, even if this means taking risks.

We've all heard the term 'mid-life crisis'. You know, the person who is okay and seemingly happy at thirty-nine, but who crumbles into a heap on their fortieth birthday. Forty seems to be a time when people take stock and re-evaluate their lives. Often, when they put their past lives under a microscope they don't like what they see. Well, why wait until you are forty to start evaluating? Start at twenty or thirty. Plan now so that when you do hit that venerable age, you aren't racked with guilt and resentment. The choices, good or bad, that you make in the years before you are forty will have an impact on your life when you do turn forty. Why not evaluate your life on a regular basis? Ask yourself 'How am I doing?', 'Am I heading in the right direction?' If not, why not? What can you do now to ensure that when you do turn forty (which may seem a long way away for some) you face the future with confidence, joy and anticipation, rather than fear, loathing and apprehension? Maybe by not recognising or taking responsibility for them, we can behave as though such choices are not really ours. But they always are.

TAKING RESPONSIBILITY FOR CHOICES

Take Sharon, for example. She was a year or two away from finishing high school. A lot of her friends were leaving school and trying their luck in the workforce. They felt school was a waste of time: all that homework, teachers, what a drag! Sharon's friends made certain choices, but many won't realise the consequences of their behaviour for a long time: months, even years, from now. Sharon knew that if she left school now, not only would her employment opportunities be limited, but she would be limiting her opportunities for further study. She stayed at school and now at least has that minimum qualification. She also managed to get into university, but has deferred for a year, while she contemplates future choices and consequences.

Although it is important to understand the complex emotional basis of many of our choices, we should never let the complexity inhibit our attempts to understand or provide an excuse for not taking responsibility for them, even in situations where the consequences may be far-reaching. The more we understand ourselves, particularly our inner selves, the more options we make available and in so doing, the less limiting, and potentially more enriching, our lives can become. For some, this may represent a daunting prospect and in some ways it is. With more choice comes the potential for more confusion but also the possibility of greater understanding.

7
De-compartmentalise your life
removing the boxes we live in

Do we all lead 'separate lives' within the one life we live? Are we a bundle of different, fragmented characters switching from one role, or compartment, to another as the situation demands? To an extent, this *is* the case. On one level, we can have a professional or work life, a family life, even a club or sports life. They all make different demands on us, and there is some 'channel-switching' from one to another. However, there is a vital common denominator between all these compartments and that is you. It's your life, and how you move from one compartment to another will have a bearing on how integrated and whole your life is.

We all live in boxes. Our homes and places of work, as well as many of the places we visit, are in many ways just elaborate boxes where the contents take on a variety of different meanings for us. We tend to compartmentalise particular rooms to fulfil particular functions, and in that sense we do a good job at keeping the rooms separate.

It's easy to segment our physical lives in this way, by having a room to eat, another to sleep, another to wash, and yet another to relax or even work in, and this makes sense. But what if our emotional life is divided up in this way? The

DE-COMPARTMENTALISE YOUR LIFE

results and implications of not having an integrated life can be quite extraordinary, as we shall see.

On the outside, and to all his friends, Phil seemed quite a remarkable person: the type who had endless energy and seemed to be involved with all sorts of activities. His friends would constantly comment about his apparent ease at switching from one thing to another while appearing a different person depending on what he was doing. While his friends had always measured Phil's success by his diverse involvements and outward achievements, Phil was becoming increasingly concerned about the way he was running his life and his apparent lack of success at maintaining an integrated inner life.

Rather than having one integrated life, Phil seemed to have several fragmented lives: a home life, a work life, a social life, a communal life, a private life, as well as a serious life and a light-hearted life. The strange thing was that they all seemed to be quite separate in the sense that it was very difficult to find the common threads running through the various separate lives. It was almost as though Phil had several different people occupying the same body, each in conflict with the other. Phil behaved like a chameleon, blending into an ever-changing landscape.

Where he was, what he was doing or who he was with always had an enormous bearing on how Phil behaved and responded. The situation he was in would always influence his manner and style of communication with others, as though his behaviour must fit certain predetermined roles. All Phil had to do was make sure he knew which role he was playing. Then he could slip into the appropriate behaviour. He made sure that he didn't confuse roles by mixing his friends and colleagues from different activities. Phil could only define himself by the role he was playing at the time ... just like an actor.

This was one hell of a way to run a life even though the pay-off must have been there in some form because he had continued to

DE-COMPARTMENTALISE YOUR LIFE

play the game for many years. The problem for Phil was that it had, over the last year or so, become increasingly difficult for him to maintain all these separate lives. The various roles were crowding out any sense of an integrated person.

Trying to compartmentalise one's life into neat and tidy boxes is the exact opposite of striving to maintain an integrated life. By contrast, the act of de-compartmentalising or integrating all the aspects of one's life is, in so many ways, the ability to bring together, recognise, reconcile and deal with all of the various and often conflicting aspects of our personality and emotional make-up. This not only makes sense but provides the basis from which we can develop our inner selves in a total sense.

At some point we have to recognise that all our 'external' lives are simply part of one life. Segmenting our lives in a way that seems convenient and allows us to spread ourselves across a range of activities does, in one sense, nothing more than deny the totality of our inner life. It is this life that, in trying to speak out in one voice, knows no boundaries or compartments of convenience.

> ✵
> We need to apply the same values and ideals to all our separate roles. The more each role flows into another by sharing common values, the more integrated we become.

If we are to gain some valuable insight into our life, we need to apply the same values and ideals to all our separate roles. The more each role flows into another by sharing common values, the more integrated we become. The compartments in our lives may still be there, but the walls are transparent and we flow effortlessly from one role to another. We shed our masks. We are no longer, for example,

DE-COMPARTMENTALISE YOUR LIFE

the hard-nosed business person who is a loving family person as well. We blur the distinction between the roles, smoothing out the highs and lows into a more level, homogenous and integrated person.

Like Phil, at some point we may well be forced to face the fact that many of the aspects of our lives that drive us to maintain the facade of separate lives come from the same 'emotional well'. This 'well' often reflects our innermost needs and desires that cut across the artificial boundaries we erect and which defy being put into neat boxes. We need to recognise the various aspects of our emotional life as a basis for understanding the connections between all the different aspects, i.e. compartments, of our life. This will provide the basis for starting to tear down the compartments and building a richer, more integrated life.

It's okay to recognise that we maintain separate lives because of needs and desires that may be served by our different activities. The difficulty arises when we become so preoccupied with the pay-off in terms of approval-seeking and rewards. We spend so much of our energy keeping these lives separate that they totally mask our ability to see the underlying one-ness of our lives.

On a macro, or wider, level we can and should view our lives as a whole. On a micro, detailed level, we do see the compartments that make up our lives, almost like cells under a microscope. It's a matter of the micro level mimicking the macro level: a little like computers that can create fractals, mathematical models defined as graphic, colourful forms. The intriguing thing about these images is that the more you zoom in on the detail, the more it mimics the overall image. So, too, should the detail of our lives mimic the overall wholeness.

8
Trust and honesty
trick or treat?

There's a lot of talk about honesty, about integrity, about 'doing the right thing'. But what do these terms really mean? Few of us are honest all the time; we all have the odd slip-up, and we all know about so-called white lies that are spoken with the best intent.

If you are going to organise your life in a more harmonious and balanced way then honesty is a crucial element. We need to be honest with ourselves and with others. Let's first take a look at being honest with ourselves.

Sometimes we fool, or pretend to fool, ourselves. We like to rationalise things we have said, things we have done. This is a way of being dishonest with ourselves. In the end it doesn't work because of the 'sleep at night factor'. We can't keep fooling ourselves, because one day, maybe tomorrow, maybe next month or next year, the truth will all catch up with us. Being less than honest with ourselves and others can also short-circuit our chance to achieve our potential. We think that because we've taken an 'honesty-shortcut' we'll achieve something a little faster. Often just the opposite is true.

Trust and honesty

Will has been working at his new job for six months now. He left school with reasonable grades, and took the job he thought he'd eventually like. But now it's just dull routine every day. He has tried to convince himself that he likes it, but really he hates it. Until he can admit to himself that he hates his job, he is being less than honest. Sure he needs the money, sure it's hard to get up and go to a job he dislikes but there is no need to keep fooling himself. Just think about what options and opportunities may exist, and explore those options before you do something rash or extreme.

If you find yourself in a situation like Will's there isn't necessarily a problem. It could be an opportunity to change an element of your life. This is where honesty comes in. Confront the situation, clearly and honestly. Don't put it off. Recognise it, accept the need to change, and understand your reasons for change.

We are often less than honest about our appearance or our health. We try very hard to avoid issues such as being overweight, or unfit. When somebody joins Alcoholics Anonymous, the first thing they say at the meeting is 'I am an alcoholic'. No more lies, no more fooling themselves. Once we admit there is a problem, we are on the way to solving it. Part of personal development is the ability to take control, to be responsible for our actions, and accept the consequences. But life doesn't have to get out of control before we take evasive action. We will be returning to this theme several times.

> ✯
> Once we admit there is a problem, we are on the way to solving it. Part of personal development is the ability to take control, to be responsible for our actions, and accept the consequences.

Another 'living lie' that is quite noticeable these days is the 'Husband's Car Phenomenon'. This is where a husband drives an expensive, safe, up-market car. He only drives to work, garages the car and drives home, while his wife, who may also be working, collecting children, doing the shopping and other running around, drives a beat-up rust-bucket. The husband 'rationalises' that he needs this car for his work, that he can't be seen to arrive at work in an older car. He may also say his wife only needs the car to collect the children and go shopping. You can no doubt think of men who drive safer, newer cars than their wives ... ask them why, and see what they say. Ego drives them, not honesty.

Another dishonest phenomenon is the 'Missing Father Syndrome'. Sometimes the previous situation and this one go together. Here a working husband and father leaves early in the morning and comes home late. Of course, the reasons can be genuine. However, husbands may use work as a convenient excuse to opt out of responsibilities. One part of life is used to mask another. These fathers miss out on a lot. Many don't see their children at all during the week. The rationalisation then is to create 'quality time', one of the most frequent clichés of recent times. Children don't understand 'quality time'; they haven't read the books and articles or seen the current affairs specials. They only understand 'quantity time'. The rest is a token contribution and a less than honest excuse. Children grow up hardly knowing their fathers, the guys who come home late from a place called 'the office', grouchy and moody, and snap at you. On weekends they'll sleep or spend some token 'quality' time with the children. Then it's back to the same old avoidance behaviour.

If you fall into this category you might need to ask yourself why are you avoiding the family? What is it that is keeping you away? Is this behaviour consistent with an honest relationship? Priorities may need to be reconsidered, and lies have to stop.

Honesty should also characterise dealings with people, friends, associates, your closer relationships, and members of the opposite sex. Being honest in your relationships will help to ensure their quality and integrity. If there is a problem you should hear about it. If you have a problem, don't hide it, or stew over it; tell the other person. Deal with the issue by getting it out into the open, then get on with your relationship, no grudges, no ill feelings. Nothing should be taken for granted.

It's important to keep in mind that honesty goes a lot further than a simplistic notion of telling the truth. Look again at the definition we began with. There's a well-known quotation from a poem by Sir Walter Scott, 'Oh what a tangled web we weave when first we practise to deceive.' The tangled webs are created by the games we play, the deceptions we put in place, the 'political' situations we create amongst friends and colleagues.

Honesty can help you to slash through the web. It will prevent you creating the web in the first place. Think very carefully about your actions and your thoughts. Are they motivated by a premise that isn't honest or well founded? Is someone going to get hurt, either physically or emotionally, by your actions? Put yourself in the other person's place, and ask if it still feels the same.

Finally, you have to really believe in the value of honesty. Once you do, it will permeate many of your attitudes. You can focus on the quality of your relationships rather than trying to cover up or remember what story you told which person. Learn to be honest with yourself and this attitude will translate into your dealings with others.

9
What are you worth?

Have you noticed that when people talk positively about someone, they often talk about what the other person has. When they talk in a negative way, it is often about what the person doesn't have. It's as if they should have things, or it's their fault if they don't, when in fact they may choose to be like that for their own reasons. You can almost draw up a catalogue of what 'popular' people have, a catalogue that provides the basis for measuring them. It generally includes a large house (or two or three), a flashy car, an apparently successful business, lots of friends (collected as if they were possessions), a magnificent boat, an art collection and so on.

> ✯
> It may be that there comes a point on the 'net worth' scale where financial wealth cannot compete with personal worth.

These possessions are not only meant to make a person feel good. They are thought to command a level of authority, as though material success of itself bestows some higher degree of authority, power and status. Of course, in one sense material possessions do bestow something more, but what are they really worth? It is also very easy to lose everything: a bad business decision, too much debt

WHAT ARE YOU WORTH?

and all the possessions may be gone. Similarly, people who don't have much may be seen as underachieving, 'worthless' people. This indicates confusion between what a person may be worth financially (and hence in status) and what they are worth to themselves or others as another human being. Sometimes there can even be an inverse relationship between what a person is worth in a material sense, and what their value to others is in an emotional or spiritual sense. It may be that there comes a point on the 'net worth' scale where financial wealth cannot compete with personal worth. In that case, money tends only to confuse or undermine the value of what you are to another emotionally, or spiritually.

Simon was the ultimate deal-doer. His latest fix was the next deal. He always needed just one more deal to keep him going. This was despite the fact that he had more money and possessions than he would ever know what to do with (or know how to enjoy or share). Simon had a few people whom he called friends, but often they got in the way of the next deal. They could never be more important than the deal itself. They could never deliver the same rewards or thrills as the deal.

Despite his ruthless manner, Simon did have one special friend, Frank, who remained loyal to him even though he too realised the importance of the deal to Simon. Frank had also done pretty well in the possessions game but he had been able to keep more balance in his life. Over the years Frank had placed a lot of emphasis on his friendships and what he could put into them. He was loyal and expected loyalty from his friends, whereas Simon found the commitment difficult.

One day, Frank's workplace was destroyed in a fire. Frank was devastated. It was so unexpected and he didn't know how he would cope. Sure, he was insured, but years and years had gone into the building of this business. He also felt responsible for his staff who would be out of work for months until his business was up and running again. It really couldn't have happened at a worse time. He turned to Simon for support and help, but Simon couldn't give it. For all his wish to help, Simon found it impossible to separate his idea of friendship from what he had. He could only think of offering things. Simon offered him his house, his boat for a holiday. Other friends offered advice and even some temporary office space. Simon offered Frank everything except his time, his presence and his understanding, which of course was what Frank needed more than anything.

In Frank's time of need, Simon was like a fish out of water. He didn't know how to respond. He could only follow his standard formula of valuing his possessions and seeing them being of value to others. Both men were devastated: Frank, because he felt that Simon could not really be there for him, and Simon, because he couldn't understand why Frank had rejected his generous offers.

In the end, of course, it may be that despite all our attempts to surround ourselves with possessions that reflect our outward success, we do little to reinforce a sense of lasting value to ourselves. It may take some crisis for us to recognise habitual patterns of behaviour and begin to change the way we value ourselves and others. The value we give others and ourselves stems from how we value ourselves as individuals, not as owners of possessions. It's what we are rather than what we have that counts, even though for many this requires a major shift in attitudes and beliefs. At some point we have to learn to believe that what we are is a constant. Our possessions are transient.

10
Being competitive
who wins, who loses?

Win at all costs. The one with the most toys wins. I'm smarter than you. I'm richer than you. My results are better than yours. I've got a better job than you. He's not as smart as me. Sound familiar? We've all been guilty of behaving like this at some time. This whole competitive game can be seen very early in children. You can often hear five-year-olds saying things like, 'I've got more toys than you' or 'My daddy's got a better car than your daddy' or 'Our house is bigger than yours.' Harnessed properly, this competitive streak can be a positive force. In moments of weakness we all like to feel that we are bigger, better and smarter than someone else we know.

But we should see this competitive behaviour for what it mainly is—futile. Competition can either massage the ego or make us feel miserable. The truth is we can always find someone who's smarter than us, or who may not be as bright as we are. There will always be people who think we are lucky, while at the same time we are thinking that someone else is lucky. It's all relative.

Some Native Americans base status and wealth not on the accumulation of riches, and who has the most, but on generosity, who gives away the most. What a different slant that would give to our lives. Modern western society tends to define who we are by what we have and what we do.

We've all been to parties or a function where somebody comes up to us and asks, 'What do you do?'(or if you are a student they may ask 'What are you studying?'). Through common experience we know that this person is asking us how we earn a living. But what are they really asking? Often they want to establish some sort of pecking order. This person wants to establish where on the socio-economic rung we fit. Are we worth talking to? Am I a brain surgeon (with the wealth and status implied)? Or do I work in the clock section of a department store (with the status and wealth that this position implies)? Often, the same pecking order can be seen amongst tertiary students. 'I'm studying medicine ... and you're only doing Arts.'

It's okay to ask someone what they do for a living if it's relevant, but not simply to establish a pecking order. Let's accept people at face value without our attitudes being 'coloured' by whether they are millionaires or mountain climbers. Finally, if someone has an occupation that he or she believes to be important, you'll find out soon enough without asking. They'll start off the conversation with a line like 'I was driving back from seeing a patient ... ' Or 'My parents just came back from Europe and ... ' Be aware of statements that seek to impress, and don't take the bait. Don't try to impress back because you are then playing their game of one-upmanship. This game can get rather messy and there are no real winners.

Nothing brings out the competitive beast in people more than possessions, the things we want to buy and own. Graham recently bought a new video-cassette player, nothing too flash, but one that will do the job

BEING COMPETITIVE

without breaking the bank. Graham's friend Richard was over later that week. When Richard saw the VCR he immediately told Graham that it lacked the features of his own player. It didn't have this, or that, and he even told Graham he had paid too much for it. Graham felt terrible. He liked his new machine, and what possible good did Richard achieve, apart from trying to establish his own status and superiority?

There is nothing to be gained by telling someone that what you have is bigger, better and costs more, nothing at all. It's just posturing and showing how insecure you are. The game of defining your self-worth through your possessions merely highlights the fact that your values and beliefs are directed more towards what you have than what you are.

Being competitive is a choice you make. But be careful. It's a merry-go-round that's very difficult to get off once you start. Car manufacturers, for example, pander to people's competitive natures. That's why there is often a choice of so many models. No sooner do you buy one model than somebody else you know has the next one up, therefore more perceived status and prestige; you obviously bought the 'cheap' one. If you are a 'player' then you'll quickly decide that the model you currently have is old. It may only be two years old and you need to move up a notch or two. At some point you have to ask yourself where will this all end? If you decide not to play the game, you instantly become 'competition-proof', which also makes you 'envy-proof'. You no longer covet that great-looking jacket, or the new mountain-bike, new roller blades or new car. You no longer feel you need to shift to a 'better' suburb just because some of your friends have. You are content with what you have, and when you want or need something else, it's unlikely you will do anything irrational, like taking on a huge debt to get it. You begin to see things for what they are.

That thought process leads on to thinking about why you want to buy, or compete in the first place. Who are you trying to impress? Your friends? Your parents? If you are true to yourself, then you don't need to prove anything to anybody. You will feel more secure when your attitudes and values reflect who you are and what is important to you, rather than when you are chasing possessions and status.

'Reflected glory' is another subtle instance of competitiveness. This is where people compete by association. That is, they like to have some of your success or status rub off on them. Take Anne and Sidney who are having some friends over. You don't know them too well, but they have invited you over anyway. Once there, you are introduced as the couple who have just built a new house in one of the more affluent suburbs. How's that for a conversation starter? Anne and Sidney are 'piggy-backing' on your perceived affluence or success. They are impressing their other friends by showing them the calibre of acquaintances they have. It's reflected glory. How often have you heard people say 'I know someone who has a Porsche', or 'My brother has a good friend who has a holiday house in France ... '? Be aware of the Reflected Glory Game. It's a game without winners.

> 'Whether you move up or down the ladder, your position is still shaky. You can only be confident when both feet are on the ground.'

Being competitive can, of course, have a healthy side in work, play and sport. The Olympic Games are all about competing and winning. First place does take the gold. At school you compete for good results, and in the workforce you compete for available jobs, and once in the job you

BEING COMPETITIVE

compete for promotion. The important thing is to keep competition in perspective.

It's okay to do well, it's okay to win. Being competitive for its own sake, and winning for the sake of winning are okay in certain aspects of life. But winning in order to see your opponents crushed is unworthy, and needing to compete and win in everything is ultimately unproductive. To paraphrase the ancient Chinese *Tao Te Ching*: 'Whether you move up or down the ladder, your position is still shaky. You can only be confident when both feet are on the ground.'

Whether we harness our competitive spirit in a constructive or destructive way will speak volumes about the type of person we are, in particular the attitudes, beliefs and values that are important to us.

11
When is a problem an opportunity?

The job interview is over. You think that you did quite well. You know you are the right person for the position: you're sure you'll be offered it. Within a few days, a letter arrives from the company. You quickly tear open the envelope. You didn't get the job. You are shattered. All your hopes were riding on this job. Is the failure a problem or an opportunity? Your first reaction is that it's a problem. Something you desperately wanted to happen didn't happen. You feel bad, your self-esteem is crushed like a piece of paper. Well, there might be another way of looking at it. It doesn't all have to be seen as bad news.

Each rejection can be an opportunity to reflect on, refine and improve yourself. An expert in sales and marketing once said 'If you are not hearing the word "no" often enough, then you are obviously not trying hard enough.' Consider getting some feedback from the person who interviewed you. Call them, or write, asking why you were rejected. That information can be very useful during your next round of interviews. You may find that you didn't seem interested enough in the job, or that you had very little knowledge about the position or organisation in question. It's important to separate you, the individual, from the

When is a problem an opportunity?

rejection. You as a person are not a failure, you just didn't get the job. The disappointment must be kept in perspective. It's also important to understand your own emotional make-up, because your reaction depends on your resilience.

A problem can become an opportunity if you respond to it in a constructive manner. Let's look at a situation where two people experience exactly the same event, but react to it in entirely different ways.

Take the case of Andrew and Ivan. They both lost their jobs within a week of each other. Andrew saw it as a real problem. He was given quite a healthy pay-out by his former employer, but he saw himself as a failure, and all the negative news around him meant that he quickly sank into despondency. Ivan was surprised that he had been retrenched. He was initially angry and anxious but soon began to treat the situation as an opportunity. Losing his job meant a re-evaluation of his career goals and his current skills and capabilities. Ivan realised that he might need further qualifications to ensure that he remains employable, and more 'fire-proof'. He spoke to his former personnel officer, who suggested that Ivan do a course to boost his computer skills, which made sense to him as he had always had an interest in computing.

We recently heard that Ivan was still actively looking for work, and he feels that his chances of securing a new position are now better than ever. Oh, yes—Andrew. He's still on the dole and hasn't been to a single job interview. He spends most of his time just thinking about his problems.

Relationships generally have a similar mix of problems and opportunities. A problem usually indicates an opportunity to sort out and clarify the situation. Problems at school or at work usually tell us something. They are lessons waiting to be learned, opportunities waiting to be unlocked. It's the old

When is a Problem an Opportunity?

> ✶ Your response to anything is in your control. You can choose to get mad, get even, or just get on with it. The choice is yours.

story of the glass that is half filled with water. The optimist says it's half full, the pessimist says it's half empty.

So often we hear people say that they are sad because of the weather, or unhappy because of something somebody did or said. But just think for a moment. Events may trigger your unhappiness, but you can choose how you want to respond. If you get a flat tyre on your bike or car, you could fume and fuss and get really mad; or you can choose to fix the tyre. Your response to anything is in your control. You can choose to get mad, get even, or just get on with it. The choice is yours.

Every day of our lives we are bombarded with choices, opportunities, distractions, good news, bad news, indeed the effects of all sorts of external events. How we respond to them will, at a fundamental level, determine what sort of life we have. If we are forever moaning about all the things that happen to us, and choose to think of ourselves as victims without any control over our lives, then our whole approach to life is likely to become very sad indeed. So, once again, it is critical to be aware of how our attitudes and beliefs shape much of our thinking and behaviour.

The challenge, in current jargon, is to become pro-active, rather than re-active. Pro-active means you initiate change and control your response. Re-active means you merely react to events, you don't control them. There are plenty of examples in office life. The pro-active person sees an opportunity to increase sales. They tell their boss who praises their initiative (initiative is a very close friend of being pro-active) in seeing that opportunity. The re-active

WHEN IS A PROBLEM AN OPPORTUNITY?

person is one who has to be told to go and seek out opportunities. These people are usually not self-motivated. They do the minimum to get by: nothing more, nothing less.

You have the opportunity of becoming the captain of your own ship, steering a course through life that is full of adventure and excitement. How you respond to the various problems and opportunities along the way will determine whether your ship sinks or proudly sails ahead. It's up to you.

12
Positive thinking
friend or foe?

Think positive. Don't worry. Be happy. It will all work out. We've heard it all before. The truth is, we can't be happy all the time. It's pointless trying to be. Happiness, like so many things in life, ebbs and flows. If you are driving somewhere and somebody smashes into your car, you are certainly not going to be particularly cheerful. If you break your leg during a skiing holiday, a friend insults you, or a friend becomes very ill, those things won't please you either. Are we saying that you can't or shouldn't strive to be happy? Are we taking a pessimistic view that everything is serious, and if you are happy then there's obviously something wrong with you? No, but there is more to feeling good about yourself than just being plain old happy.

> ✯ There is more to feeling good about yourself than just being plain old happy.

So what exactly does being 'happy' mean? The *Macquarie Dictionary* defines 'happy' as 'characterised by or indicative of pleasure, content, or gladness'. Or even 'favoured by fortune; fortunate or lucky'. If all you want to do is to be happy, then you are bound to be disappointed.

Many regard happiness as the ultimate goal of human existence. *We* see contentment, balance and peace of mind as the goal. Happiness and joy (a more intense form of happiness) flow on from these. Contentment, balance, harmony can be an enduring state of mind, happiness is a pleasant 'side-effect'. We feel happy because we are at peace and content.

There are other types of happiness that are simply transitory. We are happy to receive a birthday present; we are happy that it won't rain on a particular day. But our inner core of balance and harmony is unshaken by transitory happiness or even sadness. It's a core that remains stable within us. Without this stable core, positive thinking is merely an overlay, a cosmetic cover-up of symptoms. It's similar to a clown's make-up, a happy face on the outside ... but what lurks behind the mask? We need to create a solid foundation, a platform from which to move forward.

If you have an 'attitude problem', if you are filled with anger or resentment or if you are simply not coping, then positive thinking may offer a temporary high, an instant feel-good sensation—but it wears off very quickly. Simple positive thinking can be replaced with a range of other 'states of mind' that can help you become more self-reliant. Strength of spirit gives you the resilience to cope with the bombardment of problems large and small that we all face in our daily lives. Peace of mind is a natural outcome of this strength of spirit. You develop an inner calmness and serenity that allows you to cope ... why? Because you have an inner core that will give you sustenance. It will heighten your joy and happiness, as well as support you in times of crisis and sadness.

No single chapter in this book contains the 'secret' to achieving this state. Contentment, balance and peace of mind are a combination of many things that you, the reader,

POSITIVE THINKING

need to think about and integrate in your own life. After reading all we have to say, you should be well on your journey to achieving this state of calm in the eye of the storm. No matter what is whirling around you, you are at the centre, calm and serene, always.

There is no one answer, or a single path to achieve this. Religion, for example, gives many people solace and comfort. It can also provide you with a philosophy and guidance. You can define yourself through religion and use it as part of the fabric of your life. Books on positive thinking, and a lot of other motivational books, generally offer a quick-fix solution. You don't need the positive thinking which masks a problem, you need to work on the underlying cause, be it attitudinal or behavioural.

Mary was always being told to have a positive outlook on life. She had even once attended a talk on being positive. Things went along fine until the end of the year. Her results came through. She didn't make it into the next class. She had 'failed'. Mary was devastated. What happened to all that positive thinking? It had vacated the premises faster than a tenant owing three months' rent. Mary had no other resources to help her during this awful time. In fact, her simplistic positive attitude may even have contributed to her poor performance. She may even have deluded herself into thinking that all would be well. Perhaps she made the mistake of replacing learning and discipline with a false sense of security, the head-in-the-sand syndrome. She also didn't take responsibility for her actions.

Had she developed an inner core of strength and discipline she might not have experienced difficulties in the first place. The positive thinking made her happy on the surface, but it kept her from seeing or hearing the truth. Had she still not passed her exams, she might have handled the failure differently, possibly in a way that would have had a less devastating effect and which would have allowed her to make more rational choices about her future.

Many of us have a habit of being suspicious, or even envious, of people who seem happy or content most of the time. We tend to think of them as a little strange. Friends often say 'Why is Tom always so happy? Doesn't he have problems or difficulties?' The truth is he probably does. We all do. Unless you are dead, you'll always face challenges, problems and frustrations, but there can also be plenty of laughter and joy. It's all a product of being alive and connected to the world around you. It comes down to what's inside you, that inner core of serenity and strength that affects how you respond and react to stimuli around you. You do have a choice. You can either react in a meaningful way, or just crumble; but more of that in the next chapter.

Once you begin to deal with the underlying sources of your behaviour, you will realise that quick fixes are just that and they prevent you from dealing with the core issues. Feeling 'pumped-up', positive and gung-ho just isn't important. Being centred, balanced, in control and at ease with yourself and your world is far more important and lasting.

Part 2

Emotions and feelings

13
Feeling, recognising and dealing with emotions

In Part one of this book we examined in some detail the attitudes, values and beliefs we hold; where they come from, how they are formed and how they help to define the type of person we are.

In the same way, our emotional make-up provides a very strong basis for understanding who we are and how we are likely to feel in any particular situation. To understand ourselves more completely and gain insight into our responses, it is important to understand the nature of our emotions and feelings.

Emotions are our inner responses to events, situations, encounters, thoughts and fantasies. They manifest themselves in our feelings; those strange sensations which bubble up inside us when we find ourselves in particular situations. Our emotions cover the full spectrum of human experience and feeling; our responses can be those of love, hate, anger, jealousy, fear, aggression, lust, despair, joy, compassion, hope, pride, gratitude or sorrow. These are states of being and feeling. They are our responses to

FEELING, RECOGNISING AND DEALING WITH EMOTIONS

particular situations and often depend on our current state of mind.

At times, we tend to react to certain negative situations by trying to block off our feelings, because those feelings may seem too painful to deal with. This is a pity, because our feelings reflect and define our emotional make-up and are a rich pool to draw from. Denying them may lead to depression or anxiety.

> ✹
> If we deny ourselves anger, hate, despair or sorrow, we are equally likely to lose our ability to feel love, hope, joy or compassion with any intensity.

We have all seen a rainbow at some time in our lives. It covers the full spectrum of colours: each merging with and overlapping the next. In the same way, each of us has an emotional rainbow within us. We have the potential to feel the full range of emotions and, in doing so, obtain a much clearer understanding of our response to events and people.

One key to gaining this insight is being prepared to recognise and accept our emotional responses, regardless of whether we see them as positive or negative. This can be difficult, and is often painful and confusing. Our emotional responses may be not black or white but, like the rainbow, slightly mixed. It is important to embrace the full spectrum of the emotions we experience and not simply block them off or deny their existence. As we shall see later, there is a certain symmetry in many aspects of our lives. This is especially true in the case of our feelings. If we deny ourselves anger, hate, despair or sorrow, we are equally likely to lose our ability to feel love, hope, joy or compassion with any intensity. By 'cutting out' part of our emotional rainbow, we condemn ourselves to a life of perpetual greyness. In such a state, we go through life having only

Feeling, recognising and dealing with emotions

shallow emotional responses, whether to the most positive and joyful events or the most painful.

We probably all know people who are emotionally trapped within themselves. However hard they try, they simply can't express their feelings to others: their emotions appear to be all knotted up like a tight ball, unable to find a way out. Sometimes, people simply don't know what to do with their feelings when they have emotional reactions. Others are afraid to express emotion for fear of showing their true selves to the outside world. They don't want to be emotionally vulnerable. The fact is that emotional vulnerability is likely to be heightened when people are out of touch with their feelings.

To feel a personal and intense response to an event is a natural and important human quality. We should always be prepared to embrace our feelings, work with them, and certainly not deny their existence or our right to them. Even if we are very busy, it is important to take time to stop and become aware of our feelings during the day. Do you have feelings of contentment, hope, joy, anger? Whatever the feelings, it is important to stay with them and experience them to the full.

Your feelings are also important in providing an insight into the connections between various aspects of your life. For example, if you are reprimanded at work for something you didn't do, this will produce an emotional response. If you can at least recognise the response, you might then be able to understand the reason for it and try to see if it could be connected with another event, or piece of personal history, that may help to explain your reaction.

We all have to recognise that our emotions are an integral part of defining who we are: once we accept this, we are more able to recognise the strength of our emotions, both positive and negative. Many of our passions arise because of

Feeling, recognising and dealing with emotions

our strong feelings related to our values or beliefs and lead us to form particular relationships. The central point is to recognise the reasons for our emotional response.

It is equally important to remember that thinking and feeling are not the same. When you *feel* something, you know your reaction. If, however, you simply *think* you feel some response, it is probable that the thinking is stronger than the feeling. Once you are more aware of your feelings, you will become more aware of your inner and physical responses. Thinking that you feel something is unlikely to cause any inner response. It may simply erect a barrier to developing a clearer understanding of your emotional complexities and needs.

However, once you begin to understand what your emotions are, where they come from and what they represent and to experience the full range of feelings you are capable of, you can begin to recognise and accept that emotions belong to you and are not simply something 'out there'. This will provide you with greater insight into the type of person you are. To deny your emotions, and the feelings that result, will do little more than produce anger and maybe guilt, as we shall see in the next chapter.

14
Denial, anger and guilt

Just imagine it. A friend has been trying to insult and hurt your deepest feelings. But you have a secret weapon—emotional blockout cream with EPF 15+ (emotional protection factor), to deal with those really heavy emotional traumas. You decide to slap on some cream and within no time you not only think you are protected from the insults, you're ready to repel any other interactions which could possibly be considered emotional or a bit risky or damaging.

Experiences like this may hurt us in ways which we don't really try or want to understand and therefore at the time it seems easier to deny that we feel anything towards these people. But in doing this we end up denying our own feelings and the ability to get close to and embrace them.

It's likely that at some point in our lives we have all slapped on some EPF cream. Whether this is because of simply trying to block out some unpleasant experience which resonates negatively inside us or because there is something about ourselves which we don't want to deal with—it doesn't matter. Putting on the cream can be a very effective way of closing down our channels and blocking any chance of gaining an understanding of our feelings, or so we think. What we don't realise, however, is that unlike

DENIAL, ANGER AND GUILT

real blockout cream which blocks out things on the outside, our emotions and feelings exist on the inside and therefore no amount of cream can really prevent the 'burning' which is going on inside. So instead of recognising this burning we slap on some cream to deny that it is really happening. Patterns of established behaviour are not only generally difficult to break but we may try to deny their existence and our responses, particularly our emotional responses.

How is such denial linked to issues of anger and guilt? Quite simply, if we deny our responses to events, including our emotional reactions, the denial may make us angry. Once the anger subsides we begin to feel guilty, particularly if we have taken our anger out on others by abusing them verbally or physically without any real justification. We may also feel guilty for having allowed ourselves to be angry or for having evil thoughts. Of course, by simply trying to deny our anger, we block off any basis for understanding where the anger comes from, the reason for it, or how to deal with it more effectively in the future. We simply set up a pattern of denial which will help to keep the anger alive and unexplained for a long time. Whether we like to admit it or not, the pattern of behaviour becomes established and seems to replace the ability to deal with the denial.

> If we are prepared to acknowledge our anger we will, over time, be able to deal with the anger more effectively.

If, however, instead of completely denying our response to a particular situation or person, we are prepared to acknowledge our anger (as well as other feelings) we will, over time, be able to deal with the anger more effectively. In giving the anger a voice, we are able to understand what it represents and eventually deal with it effectively. While we

Denial, anger and guilt

may think we can effectively block our responses to negative situations which make us angry, the anger will inevitably turn inward and we will express our feelings in other ways. Unacknowledged responses have a tendency to bubble up when we least expect it because the unconscious self doesn't always wait for an 'appropriate' time to express itself.

This means that we must accept that there is nothing wrong with embracing the range of our feelings, especially when they seem negative or destructive. This can be a source of significant personal growth because in doing so we must take responsibility for our behaviour through being in touch with our feelings. Taking this responsibility will make it easier to deal with difficult people and situations and to respond as one's own person, not merely as another's object.

It is equally important to accept that, while we might really want to deal with our anger, we might find it extremely difficult to do this. Confrontations, be they with our family, friends or colleagues, generally seem very difficult occasions. Someone usually feels crushed and so if we are likely to feel guilty about directing our anger towards somebody else we probably will prefer to bottle it up or deny it completely.

Guilt can arise, not simply from hurting someone's feelings, but also from failing to do something or not being honest. It results from our awareness of something we did or didn't do that has caused pain to another and to ourselves. Akin to fear, guilt can end up causing us to slam on the brakes in all sorts of areas of life. Battered by bitter experiences, admonished for speaking our mind even when we spoke the truth, rejected when we got angry with others, we still bear the scars of the guilt we carry from a range of experiences.

Denial, anger and guilt

To move on, we must prevent guilt having such a strong presence in our lives. By recognising and dealing with those aspects of our behaviour, or events, which result in our feeling guilty, and by not denying the existence of feelings which we might find difficult to accept, we can begin the process of understanding what makes us feel guilty and why. Once we understand these aspects it will be much easier to respond in more comfortable ways and without the resulting guilt. Similarly, by demanding a level of honesty from ourselves and others in our dealings, we can reduce the occasions when we feel guilt.

In dealing with denial, anger and guilt, we must take full responsibility for our behaviour and emotions. This in turn will give us enormous insights into our own personalities and emotional needs.

15
Respect and esteem
the face in the mirror

Have you ever thought how you feel about that face in the mirror? Do you derive good feelings about yourself from within or do you tend to rely heavily on others for such feelings? Do you have a sense of fragility about yourself, as though things are tenuous and you can't find where your inner self, or centre, is located?

These feelings may be quite common when we don't have a strong sense of self. We tend to shift ground quickly: our attitudes and beliefs can change depending on who we are talking to. In this approval-seeking mode, we do not have much of a sense of self or self-respect.

There may be many reasons why a person maintains a low sense of self-respect and self-esteem: the important point is to recognise their existence and to have a strong desire to change the situation. We must be prepared to recognise and appreciate our importance to ourselves and hold ourselves in high regard before we can start rebuilding. This may include making an honest assessment of our strengths and weaknesses, focusing on things we do well and trying to be with those who enjoy our company but also validate our self-worth. It also requires us to be honest in acknowledging those of our associates who simply reinforce our feelings of low self-esteem, as though if we all do badly, it's okay. It is not okay!

It is important to remember that this program is part of your journey of discovery: this time you are learning to accept those aspects of your inner self which, for whatever reason, you find difficult to accept. You need to learn to stop punishing yourself, to become kinder to yourself, to develop a more acute sense of what is important. If we understand how our feelings affect us we have a chance of becoming a more integrated person.

Only you can do the hard inner work of rebuilding your self-esteem. That's why it's called *self*-esteem. While others can support and encourage you, it is necessary to come to terms with yourself. One of the problems in expecting others to do this work for you is that they may have different attitudes and beliefs, and you could be left even more confused and blaming yourself, further eroding your self-esteem. Even though we all feel at times that it is easier to rely on the approval of others, this will not serve us well in the long term.

Jacqui had a self-esteem problem. You could tell that the minute you saw her. She was very overweight, not just a little chubby: her weight had become a real health issue. Jacqui also surrounded herself with friends who were a similar size and shape so they were not a threat to her. They all provided the necessary comfort and validation each needed. When Jacqui was unhappy she would eat, and find comfort in food. She felt caught in a destructive cycle. The more she looked in the mirror, the more depressed she became. To comfort herself, out came the block of chocolate and so the cycle began again. There were other problems in Jacqui's life, also reflected in her image. She felt she had lost control of things around her, including her work, so she lost control of herself too. But inside Jacqui was a happier, healthier person trying to get out.

Jacqui's doctor explained the health risks she was taking. This came as a real shock and so for the first time Jacqui began to take control. A simple diet isn't the only answer, if the underlying causes are still there. As she slimmed down, she slowly started feeling a lot better about herself. This improved her self-confidence, and began a positive cycle where the more weight she lost, the better she felt. She started to deal with the problems in her life, and faced some tough challenges. As she realised that she did have some control, she began to change things in her life that were slowly destroying her. Gradually, another Jacqui emerged out of it all like a butterfly out of a chrysalis.

Self-esteem is a powerful force. An exaggerated form of self-esteem is arrogance and a negative version is conceit. There has to be a balance between healthy love of yourself (high self-esteem) and conceit and self-absorption. Nor should self-esteem be confused with external things like the clothes we wear, or the places we go to. It's a bit like body temperature: it's a constant no matter where we are or what we do. Self-esteem shines through on the dullest of days. It's there whether you win, lose or draw. It's an inner well you draw upon for your insight, courage and wisdom.

Self-esteem is linked closely with your attitudes and beliefs. They will provide a firm foundation for your sense of self to develop from your centre, not simply as an object of someone else's desire.

Your awareness of your inner self becomes an important basis for your future growth. At some point in your life, perhaps as the

> Learn to like yourself and to forgive your past mistakes. You have to live with yourself for a long time so make the whole experience worthwhile and enjoyable.

result of a crisis, you may be confronted by the pain of commencing the journey to become your own person. Whilst it may be difficult, it will be a liberating journey.

Learn to like yourself and to forgive your past mistakes, because we all make them. You have to live with yourself for a long time so make the whole experience worthwhile and enjoyable. Once you make peace with yourself you'll begin to see the world in a different way. Learn to like, love and care for that face in the mirror.

16
Love and other desires
being connected to ourselves and others

We all want and need to be loved and to feel that we are loved. Most people also feel that they want to give love to others and when they find someone who will be the recipient of their love they hope that it will be forever. However, we often fail to recognise the basis of our love and to accept that it might change over time.

Just as our needs for love and affection may change, the same is likely to be true with those who are the object of our love. If we simply assume that our love will endure forever in the same way and for the same reasons as when it started we may be in for some rude shocks.

But before we go too much further, it is important to understand what we mean by love and try to distinguish it from related feelings such as desire, passion or affection. Love in its broadest context is about being deeply emotionally connected with another person (or persons) and having a sense of attachment or devotion to another person that provides you with a level of understanding and insight into them. It also allows you to accept them for all their qualities.

We often hear people say that they love so-and-so or love their work, their car, making money. It is important to remember that while we may be emotionally connected to these things, the pursuit of them is generally more about desire or yearning, be it for a material possession or another person. This form of desire is often more closely related to lust and sexual appetite than to love. It's very easy to confuse the two, just as it is with passion, which often expresses itself as deep desire, as intense and deep love. If the passion is about genuine connection rather than power, dominance or self-interest, then it is an important part of love. In this sense, it can be enormously powerful in creating a genuine and nurturing relationship.

> Without a true emotional foundation, romantic love so often becomes stale and even destructive.

While we might say we love our car or making money, it is difficult to have a genuine, two-way relationship with such objects. We may invest a great deal of our emotional selves in such objects; we may even try to control other people through them, but the objects themselves are incapable of providing us with any love, in the sense of an emotional connection. Often we mistake such feelings for love and treat people in the same way, not as emotional beings but as objects. If we treat others in this way, we will never have meaningful, mutually loving relationships. Such relationships will almost invariably be connected with desire, which may manifest itself in wanting to control others in the sense of exerting power over them or desiring them sexually. This is often called romantic love, and is likely to be quite different from a loving relationship.

Of course, the flame of romantic love can be an incredibly potent force, propelling us to experience the highest peaks of emotional bliss. But if that's all there is, if the real emotional connections are missing, the romantic shine can quite quickly become tarnished. Without a true emotional foundation, romantic love so often becomes stale and even destructive. Once this happens it's often difficult to stop the relationship from ending up on the slippery side. And what happens then?

Even though many relationships begin with the highest of expectations, many end in a state of despair. In such cases, the object of our love may not be the other person at all. We may be more worried about ourselves and be projecting our lack of love for ourselves onto another person. We view our attempts at loving another person as a way of feeling good about ourselves, as though if we love the other it will be easier for us to love ourselves. This may work for a while— for as long as the romance endures. However, once the flame of hot passion, fuelled by desire, is turned down a little, the hard work of staying in love really begins.

As aspects of a total loving relationship, passion and desire can be tremendously enriching. As the basis for the total relationship, they can be potentially dangerous and destructive. This is why it is so important to be clear about what we mean by love.

Being in love and in loving relationships entails being emotionally connected with another person in a way which allows a strong bond to develop without stifling your own personal growth, and accepting and loving the other person as they are, not how you would like them to be.

When we feel we can no longer change those who are the objects of our love, we may become resentful. In such cases, just as our unbridled passions can drive us into wildly romantic encounters, so too our passions can turn our love into hate when things go horribly wrong or we no longer get our own way. How easy it is to blame the other, or yourself, when the romance disappears, when you feel cheated or betrayed. Passions which have been strong in love can be equally strong in hate. We may well ask how can this happen, how can the same passions and desires which took us to the top of the mountain be responsible for pushing us to such depths?

As with all of these emotional issues we have to be prepared to examine carefully the range of our inner desires and motives in order to really understand what it means to be in love and be loved. In particular, it requires us to be open and honest with ourselves in examining our intentions and the real desires underlying the relationship. If we don't know what these are, or can't work out what we want, we should listen to what the other person says to us and how they respond to our behaviour. At its very essence love is more about the need to develop strong long-term nurturing relationships in which we can feel loved and develop feelings of love for others.

Nurturing relationships are about developing a quality of love for other people which is able to transcend day-to-day barriers or one's immediate needs. They are about recognising and accepting other people's weaknesses and idiosyncrasies and wanting, even needing, to grow through the emotional connection with another. It is through such connections that we are not only able to discover things about ourselves and learn to accept them, but can then love ourselves and others more. Such relationships are likely to be filled with compassion and understanding. When we comprehend that it is this type of love that we wish to experience and nurture, then the impact on all our relationships—with partners, friends, colleagues, children, family and siblings—can be incredibly potent.

17
Levels of consciousness

Do you ever get the feeling that there are things going on beneath the surface of your life that you don't really understand and because they can't be seen you choose to ignore or deny them? Even if you recognise that there are such things going on, they may be too complex to understand and as you are caught in the middle how could you begin to understand them anyway? So often we decide not to look too deeply because it might be painful and we may find it difficult to know how to respond to what we discover. It's also interesting to see where, inside of us, these things come from.

Thoughts and feelings that seemingly bubble up from within us and carry a message for us about some event or person, often come from that mysterious place within us called the unconscious. Many people hold the view that the unconscious is something they don't have any real control over and therefore integrating it into the conscious life or trying to understand the messages it sends us is a waste of time. Yet if we are really interested in obtaining a better understanding of our total selves we need to take a lot more time to examine not just our conscious self but also what exists within our unconscious self.

It's a bit like this. Remember the last time you visited the ocean? Most of what you saw was on the surface, miles and miles of water which seemed to touch the horizon, the endless sky, birds and maybe even some boats drifting gently on the sea. Seldom do we really think about or recognise what is going on beneath the surface and appreciate that what is happening above the surface affects what occurs underneath and vice versa. The two are parts of one system. What exists above couldn't survive without what exists below.

Similarly, each one of us is a total system and part of a larger system. We each have a particular structure to our lives and, in part, this is affected by our interdependence with other people. At the same time we generally try to maintain a certain balance in our lives. Not just physical but also emotional and spiritual balance is important in order to retain a sense of well-being. But the question is how do we maintain such balance across all aspects of our life?

Physically we may exercise to keep fit and if we get sick we may choose to visit a doctor. We rely on a doctor to diagnose our physical complaint without surgery. Often this is possible but sometimes you have to 'see' what is wrong by looking inside the body.

Our emotional well-being can also be like this although it's impossible to 'see' emotional complaints in the same way as our physical ones. Like the ocean, there is an enormous richness of life going on beneath the surface, much of which we can't see at first glance, yet without proper care and attention in the form of recognising and dealing with what is going on deep within us, we can end up just as unwell or neglected as anything that exists on the surface.

In looking at your emotional life have you ever wondered why you react in a particular way, or why certain events or people cause a certain reaction in you? Have you ever caught yourself daydreaming and then wondered what it meant? Have you been thinking quite intently about one thing when, as if from nowhere, some other seemingly unrelated thoughts entered your head? Or have you been somewhere for the first time but have a strange feeling that tells you that you have been there before? It seems that a lot of what happens in our lives does so at an unconscious level and is then constantly brought into the realm of our consciousness, which in turn influences our response. In other words, events, thoughts or memories seem to reside in our unconscious and then rise to the conscious level, causing us to react in ways we sometimes find peculiar or simply don't understand.

We seem to spend a lot of time trying to deny or close off access to our inner emotional worlds. We pretend either they don't exist or that they are separate from us. In so doing we close off all dialogue with ourselves about our inner lives. The effect of this is that gradually, maybe even imperceptibly, we lose touch with our emotional world as well as with the intuitive abilities which can have a profound impact on our insight into who we are and the emotional needs and responses we have. Why is it so important to understand our emotional complexities? Because, as we have seen, in a very real sense they, together with our attitudes, values and beliefs, define who we are.

Just as there are connections between the earth, sea and sky and the channels between them are constantly open, so too is it critical to keep the channels between our unconscious and conscious worlds open. So often our responses to certain events or people may be based simply on trying to please others, to avoid conflict or merely to look good. Whatever the reason, to rely simply on a conscious reaction without reflecting on your inner reaction and integrating this with your 'normal' response, is to fail to express your complete self. Just as exploring the vast richness of the oceans can be tremendously exciting and exhilarating, so too can the challenge of exploring the hidden wonders of our inner emotional selves. We may find that the feelings, thoughts and images that rise from the unconscious to become part of our rational thoughts are like the waves rolling onto the shore and lapping against the giant rock faces that jut out from the cliff wall, gradually wearing the rocks away. The more we are prepared to be open and listen to our 'inner waves' the more we are able to let our inner selves lap against our daily conscious lives to the point where we are likely to be more in touch with ourselves and, as a result, become a more integrated person. Our 'inner waves' can take several forms. The dreams which we so often dismiss as irrelevant, generally provide important insights and connections with sudden flashes and events we think happen coincidentally.

> The unconscious self really is quite amazing if we could only bring ourselves to go there 'consciously'.

The unconscious self really is quite amazing if we could only bring ourselves to go there 'consciously'. We can spend so much time roaming around and exploring its vast richness and bringing back to our conscious lives material which will not only empower us but also help us to define who we are and how we wish to relate to the outside world.

Just as you explore on the beach, rummaging around to look for interesting things, holding on to some and discarding others, so you can explore your unconscious self. You don't have to use or keep everything you find but at least, by going there, you will discover and understand fascinating things about yourself. What you then choose to bring to the surface and use in your conscious life is, like so many other things in life, very much a matter of your choice.

18
Our emotional choices
dealing with life's dilemmas

Have you ever noticed that things aren't always as they appear? The harder you try to do something, the worse it becomes. The more you look for a rational or logical explanation, the more confusing things seem. Often life appears full of such paradoxes or contradictions. We wish to go in one direction but something in us is operating at another level to push us in a different direction.

At the same time have you ever been aware (if you looked carefully at your behaviour and the various aspects of your life) of the way that symmetry plays an almost universal role? Symmetry is the idea that everything is divided into two halves: for example, there is an action and a reaction; a statement and a response; or a feeling within us that has an outward expression. If we oversleep, we will be late; if we don't exercise, we won't be fit; and so on. We need to create an awareness that everything we do in our lives has a certain type of symmetry attached to it, so that we can consider what the consequences of our particular actions might be.

The same is also true when it comes to issues that have an impact on our relationships, our desires, our career choices. In all of these facets of our life, the choices we make, as well as our behaviour, have an uncanny symmetrical quality, even if we are unable to see or understand it at first.

In our relationships, for example, choosing to maintain a hostile, aggressive stance with people will directly affect how they perceive and respond to us. If we are highly manipulative, political or distant from others, our behaviour will also elicit a certain response from others. Contrast this with the situation where we are committed to caring, nurturing and emotionally rich relationships. It is as though once we decide to behave in a particular way, we establish the basis for symmetry of the relationship to evolve. Of course, the symmetry tends to work in both directions: once there is an action and a reaction, that reaction will lead to another action, initiating a cycle. It is important that once the cycle is established, particularly in a relationship, it is not simply an established pattern, but based on what we really desire from that relationship.

Even though they can be very confusing, paradoxes also occupy an important place in our lives. They can tell us a great deal about ourselves, including our inner conflicts, as well as about unresolved problems which may exist more at an unconscious level but which keep coming to the surface because they have not been dealt with and resolved.

Paradoxes exist at the individual level, as well as at communal and national levels. For example, at the national level we talk about creating peace yet everywhere we look there seems to be more conflict and violence. We talk about solving our economic problems and making our societies more equitable and caring, yet the realities of our daily lives often belie this dream. Similarly, we might talk about wanting to have more rewarding and nurturing relationships with family and friends, yet sometimes our actions are quite different. This may lead us to question whether we really want these things or not, or whether they are a manifestation of our collective 'dark side' running a very different agenda. The more self-knowledge we have, the greater our capacity to recognise and reconcile the symmetry, paradox and conflict in our lives.

> The more self-knowledge we have, the greater our capacity to recognise and reconcile the symmetry, paradox and conflict in our lives.

In the end, symmetry and paradox teach us to be open with ourselves and alert to emotional responses and patterns of behaviour which we do not fully understand. By being prepared to dig somewhat deeper and explore what lies so elusively below the surface we may be able to make the sort of connections that will help to influence our behaviour and our interactions with others in a positive way which acknowledges our inner needs.

As we say throughout this book, it's very difficult to deal with just one aspect of your life without trying to understand the connections in other areas.

19
Insight, wisdom and courage

Have you ever met somebody you thought displayed incredible wisdom and insight? The sort of person who could evoke certain feelings in you, a real warmth, closeness or calmness. When they spoke they touched you on the inside in a nurturing and empathetic way.

Such people seem to come into our lives very rarely, but when they do, they generally have a profound and enduring impact on us. Such people often have an ability to make clear what seems particularly complex. They can convey their message in a way which reflects how they think and feel and which carries with it a sense of their own integrity.

It may be that such people have been humbled by personal struggles and this has become the source of their insight and wisdom. For them, insight, which is the ability to understand oneself and one's life, through perception and observation, has come not by analysing everything and everyone around them but by understanding their own struggles and emotional complexities and arriving at an integrated position.

In our attempt to become complete individuals we must reflect on who we are and decide what things are important to us. It is also essential that we stop being constantly judgemental of the actions of ourselves or others. Blaming other people for our being what we are blocks off the ability to learn anything from our experiences, and simply reinforces our established patterns of behaviour and response.

From an early age, we tend to develop a certain structure and way of behaving and responding to others. When we are young, it may be difficult for us to exercise much control over our responses or patterns of behaviour. However, as we get older, we have to begin to take responsibility for who we are and the kind of person we want to become. This is where insight, wisdom and courage play a tremendously important part in our lives, particularly our emotional lives. If, as adults, we want to change aspects of our life, we must be prepared to learn from our previous behaviour.

> The process of understanding oneself is an ongoing journey—it *is* the journey.

Insight provides us with the ability to examine our behaviour in an attempt to understand what it means, how it connects with other aspects of our life and what the pay-off is.

Once you can recognise that you would like things to be different, the changes that you can bring about are likely to be ongoing but occur incrementally. It requires courage to make changes: to face your own pain (even danger) without fear. That is why people often stay with established patterns. Courage also means being prepared to evaluate what really matters in your life and to become your own person by undertaking the arduous task of discovering your own identity and living your life accordingly. The process of understanding oneself is an ongoing journey—it *is* the journey. So, if you are looking for fast, one-stop, cure-all answers, you are unlikely to be prepared for the long haul which genuine insight requires.

If, however, you have reached the point where particular aspects of your life no longer feel right and as a result change is required, the insights you will acquire along the journey are likely to accumulate and become the source of your own inner wisdom: that ability to develop sound judgement and perspective in a way that conveys a deep understanding of your inner life and needs.

> ✷ The fact is that nobody can become 'wise' for you, just as nobody can know you as well as you can know yourself.

Such wisdom will free you, at least in part, from the pain of change, from the past patterns of behaviour and the perceived need to slavishly follow others or external 'cures'. Wisdom and insight are important, not only as qualities in themselves, but because of what they reveal to you about yourself; they will bring you more in touch with your inner life: a closeness that will make a tremendous difference to how you relate to people and situations.

In particular, you may no longer feel so caught up or obstructed by trivia or hype: you may be far less preoccupied with what others say or think about you, because you derive a greater sense of well-being from following your own path. Developing insight will certainly help you understand your major priorities and needs, especially in the context of your emotional development.

In choosing to follow a path dedicated to gaining insight, don't be tricked by those who try to convince you that the process is quick or easy. Many people revert to old patterns precisely because change is hard, painful and slow. But this is the only way to achieve lasting growth. If there were quick

INSIGHT, WISDOM AND COURAGE

and simple answers, we would all be wiser and more insightful.

The fact is that nobody can become 'wise' for you, just as nobody can know you as well as you can know yourself, especially your inner self and needs. You have to embark on, and travel through, your own individual inner journey. As you do, you may well surprise yourself in the sense of being able to deal with people, situations or emotions which previously you found difficult to handle. By trying to understand these things in your own way, you will gain further insight that also becomes the basis for growing self-confidence.

Everyone has their own story to tell: only you can tell yours in a way that reflects the insight and wisdom you have accumulated throughout your journey.

Part 3

Learning, thinking and planning

20
Planning your life
developing your personal mission statement

What is a mission statement? Normally we tend to think of a mission statement as something associated with business. It sets out a statement of corporate values, objectives or a code of behaviour an organisation wishes to follow. Whilst it can be serious, it can also include items such as 'Have Fun'. The mission statement sets out guidelines that are generally beyond simply making a profit, and selling widgets. It often establishes the tone and philosophy of the organisation, as well as setting a higher purpose.

Individuals can also have mission statements, as can families, schools, sporting clubs, even charities. In fact, any individual or group of people can develop a mission statement as a

> So, how do you develop your own mission statement? How do you plan your life? How much should you plan and how much should you leave to chance?

set of guiding principles which link the people in an organisation in their aim for a common set of goals.

So, how do you develop your own mission statement? How do you plan your life? How much should you plan and how much should you leave to chance? We would begin by saying that it's impossible to plan your life in minute detail. It's impossible because there are so many factors and variables that come into play. You need to leave room for spontaneity. You need to allow for unexpected things to happen such as a friend saying 'Let's go to Egypt to explore the pyramids', or 'Let's take a year off after college and travel … ' Then again, you could always plan to include items such as these in your Grand Plan, as part of your mission statement, if they are important to you.

The task of preparing a mission statement has several important components. Firstly, it involves establishing certain guiding principles by which to run your life. These should be in keeping with the type of person you are, your emotional nature, your talents and your priorities. Secondly, it will contain a set of objectives or goals you would like to achieve and an overall plan. These should be in harmony with your guiding principles. Finally, you will need to periodically review the plan and revise it in the light of changes to your priorities or values.

When you begin, you need to ask yourself what sort of life you would like to lead. Do you fancy yourself as an academic, an explorer, an artist, an architect, or what? You need to have some idea of where you are going if you are to get there. The important aspect of putting some sort of framework into place is that it helps you make choices along the way that are consistent with your overall plan. What you are trying to avoid is reaching the age of fifty and thinking that maybe you should have done something else when you were a student; or regretting that you didn't take that job offer overseas. Now is the time to sow the seeds for your future life. Now is the time you can make a difference. (Look back to chapter 6 on choices and consequences.)

You do have a choice to either make things happen, or let things happen. You can become a key player in your life, or you can take a back seat and see what happens. You can keep alert for opportunities, and look out for lucky breaks. A lot of wonderful things can happen to you by chance, things that can change your life. But more of that in Part five.

Let's assume that you have established an overall framework and a direction you would like your life to take. What happens next? If you need further study or other qualifications, you need to follow up with some research about the courses you need to take. You might also want to find out if there is a place where you can study overseas, and so combine an overseas qualification with some travelling. If you are looking at a career shift, talk to people who are already working in that area, and do some thinking and planning beforehand; it could save you time, trouble and money later.

Begin by making a list of values that are important to you and things you would like to do. Write down a list of goals that you would like to achieve. You might also want to write down where you would like to live, or the organisation, country or place that you would like to work in, the sort of career direction that you would like to take. This is just a personal list that nobody else has to see. You'll find it quite fascinating that all sorts of plans you didn't know you even had will emerge on the page. They'll appear as if they were written in invisible ink which slowly materialised on the page. Simply writing these things down is not only a valuable discipline but will focus your attention and give your plans credibility and reality. Your personal mission statement doesn't necessarily have to be 'engraved in

Planning your life

marble'. It can and will change and be adapted, just as you will change and adapt over time. But above all it will be your personal mission statement, a reflection of what is important to you.

It's important to put a considerable amount of effort into this sort of thinking and planning. You may discover all sorts of things about yourself. The planning can define and refine your own focus in terms of what is and isn't important. The plan is a guide, a map which you can follow. If you don't achieve some of the goals set out in the plan, that shouldn't stop you. Try to learn why that goal wasn't achieved at that time. If it is still important and possible, you may have to revise the goal or approach it in a different way. Your mission statement will instil some confidence in you by providing a point of focus, and a direction in which to pour some energy.

A final point. There have been plenty of successful people who seem to act and behave as if there were no map, as if their success just happened, because they got lucky. Don't believe it. Whether it's the teenager playing piano and dreaming of becoming a rock star, or the young adult playing with blocks and dreaming of one day putting up a real building, it's likely a mission statement is there in one form or another.

When you are heading out on the big journey of life, who's going to be better off, the one with map or the one without?

21

Structure, strategy, goals
which comes first?

There is no doubt that we all have lots of structure in our lives—structure in our homes, in our work, in our relationships. In fact, everywhere we look there is structure. It is hard to imagine life without it. How could we function at work or at home if there were no structure, no laws, no procedures, no consistency or predictability? Most of us would find it very difficult to exist.

One of the problems is that often the structures we put in place seem to end up dominating and running everything we do. We can become prisoners of our structures. Once a structure is in place it may be very difficult to change. This is often because we don't really understand how it got there in the first place. But generally once it's there it seems to have a life of its own. It's like the uninvited guest who just arrives and outstays their welcome.

> One of the problems is that often the structures we put in place seem to end up dominating and running everything we do.

Structure, strategy, goals

In this sense the structures we put in place can, if we're not careful, limit our freedom, especially our inner freedom, and inhibit what we really want to do and achieve in our lives. Many of us have dreams, plans and goals of what we would like to achieve but we're anxious that in order to achieve these things we have to change too much. We may have to alter our structures because they are not appropriate to our new goals. At the same time it is very easy to feel comfortable with our structures. They can deliver an enormous amount in the way of security and predictability, but seldom do they deliver our dreams, or enhance our strategies.

Indeed, even though we can only achieve our strategies and goals if we have the appropriate structures in place, the goal and the strategy must always come first: the appropriate structure will follow.

For years, Susie had made a job of refining the various structures in her life and becoming increasingly discontent in the process. She often wondered whether there was more to her life than the mere form of her life. Opportunities seemed to be passing her by, which was surprising because she really wanted to do well and realise her dreams. She couldn't understand what was holding her back until one day she was approached by a firm that had heard much about the work she had done. This organisation offered Susie the chance of a lifetime, a major career progression as well as an opportunity to visit new places and mix with people who shared similar dreams.

Susie was initially terrified by the prospect of moving jobs and having to change structures. How could she cope with such dramatic changes? After all, her life had developed a nice predictable flow, even though the structures were no longer delivering the goals Susie wanted to achieve.

Once she realised that continuing in the same structure would simply hold her back, and that this was no longer what she

Structure, Strategy, Goals

wanted, she accepted that it was necessary to change the structures. Having faced this inevitable choice she accepted the challenge of her new position and began the process of changing the structures in her life.

This was a long, often anxious and difficult process, requiring Susie to examine the underlying reasons for the structures she had put in place and in turn to let go of many old habits and self-imposed restraints. But once she had made the choice (which was hers to make) that she wanted a different life and she wanted to achieve some of her higher goals, she could begin to change the structures which had dramatically limited her life.

In changing her life, Susie had realised that in so many areas structure follows strategy. In other words, we need to first work out what we want (the goals), be it at home, at work, in other pursuits or relationships. We then need to think about the strategies to achieve them; then about structures which will be consistent with achieving our strategy and goals.

Susie now believes that the opportunity she was given represented an important milestone in her life. It required her to make significant changes and take several risks which were things she was not used to doing. But the choice to change strengthened her in many ways, not the least in providing her with a deeper understanding of herself.

Of course, it is okay to have a tight structure with all its limitations as long as this structure delivers what is important to you. But it may not be okay if the structure drastically inhibits the fulfilment of your strategies; if it constricts and limits the possibilities and dreams that you have set for yourself. No structure is important enough to end up destroying our dreams or ruining our strategy. If we have such structures in place, we owe it to ourselves to examine them and re-assess the basis for the choices we have made.

22
Mentor worship
from hero to zero

It has often been said that we learn by imitation; by modelling our behaviour on others. Some examples of such modelling include the way young people imitate their parents, siblings or favourite music and TV idols. As we develop, we often take on other role models. They may be teachers, work superiors or others we meet at some stage, and we choose them because they display qualities or characteristics that we admire and aspire to possess.

A mentor is someone whose advice and wisdom we trust; they can be highly influential in our lives, in both a positive and a negative sense. Cults and other groups frequently have as their leaders mentors or 'gurus' who are more interested in controlling and demanding things from their disciples than in guiding and teaching them. These 'mentors' have another agenda and we need to be wary of them. If you are lucky, a person of repute and influence may elect to become your mentor. This could be a wonderful opportunity. But you must decide for yourself if this mentor would be the right one for you.

Originally, true mentors or masters were people who had undertaken an enormously difficult, often painful, emotional and spiritual journey, as a result of which they had developed themselves to the point where they were not interested in power or controlling people. They were concerned with the process of enlightenment—gaining real insight into themselves and their world. These mentors also understood the very great responsibilities which they shouldered and were aware of the harm they could do if they abused the influence they possessed.

In assisting others with their spiritual journey, mentors are able to demonstrate deep compassion, connection and involvement with their students, balancing the students' need for love and discipline. Most importantly, true mentors are caring guides who want to help their students find their own way, and who will never seek to control the students. No-one can acquire insight for another person. Just as good coaches inspire their teams, mentors will be happy to pass on their knowledge and wisdom but will want to leave it to the students to grasp its significance and integrate it into their lives in a way which is meaningful to them. Some students, however, are looking merely for quick answers, and expect their mentors to do the hard work for them. Such students may be lazy, not committed to real personal and emotional growth, being more concerned with the acquisition of material possessions.

> Don't blindly accept everything a mentor may share with you. Keep an open mind, and feel free to question their advice.

There are also people who have been badly hurt in their youth by those whom they thought they could trust. They trusted those who had held themselves out as mentors, and said they could 'help' achieve what their protégés wanted from life. When you are confused and lacking self-confidence, you might believe such people can provide real insight and wisdom into your world. All you have to do is sit back and trust them. If you do, you may find that these mentors are able to deliver nothing except a lot of hollow words and advice.

Don't blindly accept everything a mentor may share with you. Keep an open mind, and feel free to question their advice. If your questions aren't answered to your satisfaction, you may not have a suitably caring mentor.

If you have a mentor, it might be as well to ask yourself a few questions. Are they being nice to you simply in order to satisfy some need or agenda of their own? Are they genuinely interested in your well-being or are they just pushing their own barrow? Do they want to control or influence you so that you become one of their 'disciples'? When the relationship enters a difficult patch, will they be prepared to stick with you and help you work through the difficult issues, or will they simply abandon you? Are they motivated by some higher principle, conveyed by consistency in the way they act, talk and behave?

The fact is that the mentors who are likely to have the most positive influence on our lives (often without their even being aware of it) are those who encourage and guide us with insight but insist that we take not only the final decision but also responsibility for our own thoughts and actions. In this sense, the real role of the mentor is very much akin to a 'tour guide', coach or instructor. Such a person is present with us on our journey and can provide a commentary or some useful insight into the difficult events or situations we encounter, especially if we seem confused or stuck, and unable to see our way out clearly. In such situations, a mentor who has 'been there' can provide an enormously valuable perspective as well as genuine emotional support to help us arrive at the decision which resonates most comfortably within us.

MENTOR WORSHIP

While it is okay to seek the advice, guidance or support of a mentor, it is important that you make sure that such a person acts in a way which allows you to retain complete responsibility for your decisions. They should actively encourage you to determine the course of your own life, allowing you to become your own hero.

23
Knowledge, intelligence and wisdom

So, you ask, what's all the fuss about? What is the difference between knowledge, intelligence and wisdom? People seem to use these terms interchangeably, as if all three were the same.

Let's begin with some definitions so we can be clear about the terminology.

'Knowledge' involves specific information about a subject. It is also about awareness, consciousness or familiarity gained from experience or learning. Knowledge is also about feelings, facts or experiences known to a group of people.

'Intelligence' is the capacity for comprehending; it's also about the ability to perceive and understand meaning.

So where does wisdom fit in? Wisdom puts the two together. It is the ability to think and act using intelligence and accumulated knowledge.

But we don't want you to get the wrong impression here. These elements need to be blended with some compassion and creativity. Wisdom is also about constantly developing our understanding of how our inner world relates to the outer world and being empathetic to the inner world of others. There is nothing particularly impressive about simply accumulating facts. The knowledge and wisdom you

Knowledge, Intelligence and Wisdom

acquire along the way can be very helpful to you: it can form the 'backbone' of your entire being. But you still need more. Apart from self-awareness and understanding yourself better, you also need an outlet for self-expression either within your job or chosen career or outside it.

Debbie is an excellent lawyer. She is well respected and derives a lot of satisfaction from her work. Recently she started to feel that something was lacking; that she needed to balance the intellectual pursuits of her work with something quite different. One day, she was driving with her family through a rainforest which was about an hour's drive from her home. She looked at the ferns and the undergrowth and saw how cool and refreshing it looked: all those different shades of green, the textures, the way the light filtered through the leaves. At that moment a hobby was born. Over the next few weeks, Debbie made some inquiries about creating a fernery. She found an area of her garden that had previously been neglected and had the perfect amount of shade. Over the next twelve months she watched her fernery grow. It was lush, cool and green, like a miniature rainforest in her own garden. She spent several hours there every week, working with the soil, pruning dead branches, planting other shrubs nearby. The fernery became a form of sanctuary for Debbie: she could think quietly about things, yet be involved in some physical activity. It gave her that extra balance she had been seeking.

You may not be interested in a fernery, but this example illustrates how knowledge, intelligence and wisdom need to be balanced. By reading this book, we hope you are gaining some knowledge and wisdom about your inner self, but tempering that with some other interest or hobby. This might be playing sports, or a musical instrument, stamp collecting or even model-building. Pursuing your hobby will put you in contact with others who share your interest and this helps to put other parts of your life into perspective. You become less obsessed with career or job: you can focus your mind on other interests and the benefits are real and enduring.

This balance can help us understand how we feel about ourselves and others just as we understand the outer world of school or employment.

It often seems that we grow up with a poor sense of self, with lots of knowledge but with extreme difficulty in relating to people or dealing with our own emotional needs or failings. Our factual knowledge becomes a substitute, a crutch to lean on.

Knowledge, intelligence and wisdom are far more powerful when they are applied to an understanding of both the outer and inner worlds, enriching not only our own life but also the lives of others.

24
Perceptions and reality
what is the difference?

Have you ever heard somebody say that there is no reality, only perceptions? If you think about this statement you may find more than a little truth in it. If you take a moment to examine many of the important areas of your life you might be surprised to discover how much of your thinking as well as your reactions and feelings are driven by your perceptions rather than the reality of the situation.

To others, the way we appear, talk, dress, even interact, creates certain perceptions about the sort of person we are. The same is generally true when we observe other people and situations. We tend to go along with certain perceptions of people regarding what they're like, what they'll think of us and how they may respond to us. Such perceptions may or may not be accurate. Quite often they may simply be unconsidered. These perceptions may then lead to an emotional reaction based on years of presuming, for example, that we know what another person thinks of us, but the perception may not be the reality at all.

It follows that our inaccurate perceptions about other people, about our career prospects, our attractiveness, our ability to make a contribution, can have a negative effect on our emotions, and can indeed become our reality.

It is very important to be aware of this and be able to analyse our perceptions of situations, to examine our emotional responses and to determine whether these responses are simply feeding negative perceptions which determine our reality.

An important aspect regarding perceptions is related to fear: fear of rejection, of being punished or reprimanded for not being good enough or for doing a poor job. So often, if we consider what the worst possible outcome might be, we may come to understand the part perceptions play in creating situations which have no real foundation.

Of course, whilst we often tend to think in terms of perceptions which have a negative influence on our thinking and reactions, the reverse can also be equally true. We might actually perceive ourselves and others to be doing a good job at work or wherever, to be a friendly type of person, and one who is capable of making a worthwhile contribution to a task or organisation. As long as these perceptions are well grounded and based on an integrated and honest view of ourselves and others, they can propel us in a way which helps to create a very positive reality in our daily lives. Such perceptions can also be reinforced by how others view us and the way we view and treat other people. Do we look forward to or fear meeting or talking with others? If we fear such encounters, do these fears have any grounding in reality, or is it something in the other person that causes fear in us? In such situations, it may simply be our perceptions rather than reality.

Rhonda had often experienced difficulties separating her perceptions of what people thought about her from the reality. When she was a young girl, her parents

Perceptions and reality

had made her dress in funny costumes and perform in front of friends. The friends viewed such dressing up and performing as rather silly and nonsensical and consequently came to regard Rhonda in that light. These memories and impressions remained with her, and she had always believed that people perceived her as silly, unattractive and unlikely to amount to much. Such thoughts influenced her perceptions of herself and, over time, had an impact on her attitudes and beliefs as well as the choices she made.

Years later, as a young woman in her twenties, she still held onto these perceptions, especially the belief that everyone had a low opinion of her. One day, however, she met someone who for the first time began to talk to and treat her differently from the way others had. This person didn't think she was silly at all but perceived her as a talented young women. Over time, Rhonda began to examine why this person saw her so differently. She began to examine her own perceptions and assumptions and why she had held the views she did. She came to recognise that most of the views she had of how others saw her were ill-founded and based on negative perceptions rather than facts. Rhonda gradually recognised and accepted that if she could change her perceptions of herself, she might be able to change her reality and bring greater feelings of contentment to her life.

So why is it that perceptions can be stronger than reality? How is it that the strength of what we may feel or think about how others perceive us can be greater than the reality? What can we do to change the negative perceptions and gain greater control over our choices and responses? If we think the perceptions are not valid, do we still want to perpetuate them?

False perceptions regarding a situation or another person often come from a superficial encounter. (This is what jumping to conclusions is generally all about.) In order to understand a person's reality we have to take the time and effort to gather information and understand what they are really like. In part, this requires us to recognise the difference between jumping to conclusions and really trying to understand what the other person is saying and why they behave in the way they do. This in turn requires us to be much more in tune with what others say and how they respond to us. Of course, once we are interested in finding out how our own perceptions are formed and how they are perpetuated, the quality of our life and relationships is likely to improve.

> In order to understand a person's reality we have to take the time and effort to gather information and understand what they are really like.

25
Learning from our experiences
breaking familiar patterns; establishing new ones

The experiences we accumulate throughout life can often seem to be something of a mixed blessing. They can keep us moving along the same groove or can help propel us into new areas of discovery and activity. Developing insight into when we are moving in the grooves of our previous experience and when we should break out of such patterns is critical to allowing us to move forward.

Patterns of behaviour and experience are established in nearly every area of life—in our relationships with family, friends, colleagues, at work and at home. Even in social settings, patterns of behaviour and responses become well established and, once established, often seem difficult to change. The patterns of behaviour, which may include how we perceive others and ourselves and how we respond in particular situations, tend to reflect the structures we

LEARNING FROM OUR EXPERIENCES

establish for ourselves. Many of these patterns can become comfortable. Even those which may appear to be manipulative or destructive can, in their own strange way, be comfortable. Old habits indeed die hard. Just as we may be attached to an old coat which no longer protects us and should be thrown out, often we find it impossible to discard old familiar habits and patterns of behaviour. However bad they are, they may seem safe and preferable to something totally new and foreign. In such cases, change can sometimes seem more difficult than remaining with the old patterns.

In establishing patterns of behaviour we often tend to reinforce negative behaviour and thereby reinforce feelings of low self-worth. We may get used to feeling that we aren't good enough, don't deserve or can't expect any better. Too often such feelings end up becoming a self-fulfilling prophecy.

Patterns of behaviour are often strongly established when we are young. We may have gone through our school years without enjoying the experience. Perhaps this led our teachers and parents to think that we would never amount to much. So guess what happened? We didn't get high grades and didn't get into university; we simply fulfilled their low expectations (see chapter 5). Such patterns can follow us into careers where, instead of getting the job we want, we get the one we think we deserve. In relationships the same can be true. Indeed our whole life may be run by familiar patterns which, surprisingly, we may not even recognise as familiar, repetitive or damaging.

Old patterns continue for a number of reasons and are likely to continue even when we think we have dealt with them because we fail to come to grips with what the patterns represent to us at an emotional level. We might also feel that we don't have sufficient control over our lives

LEARNING FROM OUR EXPERIENCES

to do much to change established patterns. However, once we start to examine our past behaviour, understand it and recognise the nature of our own needs and desires we can begin to understand the basis of previous actions and behaviour.

A further complication with learning from mistakes is that it seems that quite often the experiences we learn from are difficult or painful and we may prefer to forget them. So in trying to suppress or deny them, we deny ourselves the opportunity to learn anything from them. The reality is that it is only by introducing some kind of circuit breaker such as an ability to understand the underlying issues that we can begin to break familiar patterns and move on.

The process of change tends to be very difficult and requires real commitment and courage. If it were easy everyone would simply learn from their past experiences, change their patterns of behaviour and have the sort of life they dream of. Very often it is difficult to recognise or accept that there are familiar patterns at work. Many people seem to accept that their lives have a certain established pattern which they can't do anything about. It's as if some outside force is controlling them, so they tell everyone, and convince themselves, that they are powerless to change things.

Such behaviour may mean that instead of making progress towards a better life by learning from the past to create our future, we simply move into damage control. We've probably all heard people say that they are lucky that things aren't a lot worse and that if they just keep on following the old formula then at least not too much else is likely to go wrong. Even though there may not be too much moving backward in this approach, there certainly won't be any moving forward. Like a mouse in a wheel, you may experience some activity, but in the end you've really travelled nowhere.

Learning from our experiences

> Learning to recognise and deal with established patterns is an important part of the journey each of us must take. There is no easy answer.

How does all this happen? How do we get ourselves into these grooves of behaviour and how can we learn from our experiences to move on and fulfil more completely our hopes and desires?

Learning to recognise and deal with established patterns is an important part of the journey each of us must take. There is no easy answer, but there are certain things we can do to facilitate change.

We must be prepared to:
- take full responsibility for our actions;
- deal with our feelings, however difficult or painful this may be;
- understand the nature and causes of past behaviour (and its pay-offs) and be prepared to make hard choices;
- let go of old fears;
- recognise the impact that such problems of behaviour have in holding us back;
- review our attitudes towards ourselves and others;
- review our priorities;
- examine our relationships with others as well as how we treat ourselves;
- think creatively and constructively about the sort of future we want to create for ourselves;
- think about how we want to live—emotionally, spiritually, physically and intellectually;
- abandon the excuses that we use to justify perpetuating destructive behaviour;
- stop blaming others for causing our behaviour or causing us to repeat patterns of behaviour.

If we are serious about change and breaking familiar

patterns, we need to begin by examining many of the above factors which tend to hold us back. We need to begin, however tentatively, the process of shedding the attitudes and habits which are inconsistent with the sort of future that we wish to create. We need to create new attitudes and habits which will lead us into the life we want.

It will also be important to recognise that in the end you will be replacing one type of structure and behaviour with another because if we examine our lives, we will find that they all have a certain structure, pattern and rhythm to them. However, in reconstructing your life by breaking familiar patterns you may be more inclined to build new patterns or structures that mirror your inner desires, rather than simply following past patterns or responding to the wishes of others.

Inevitably you will come to realise that changing patterns of behaviour is a long and difficult journey. It involves dealing with underlying problems and their causes, which are about as far away from quick-fix solutions as you could imagine.

26
Priorities and focus
the secret ingredients

First things first. Now that you begin to glimpse the way ahead, what are your priorities? What's important to you right now? What's important to you in terms of your own development and growth? Very few of us bother to ask ourselves these questions, because the answers aren't easy to arrive at, and also, the answers could reveal chinks in our armour. Perhaps you don't know or don't think you know what is important to you, or what sort of priorities you should be looking at.

> ✭
> What you need to determine is what is important for you, not what others think is important.

Everybody naturally has different priorities because everybody has different desires and needs. What you need to determine is what is important for you, not what others think is important. You need to work out your own agenda.

Your priorities should also be a reflection of the mission statement and plan that we discussed in chapter 20 and the choices you have identified. Your priorities shouldn't necessarily be career driven. A priority doesn't have to be,

PRIORITIES AND FOCUS

'I'm going to be an accountant' or 'I'm going to become an actor'. The test is their importance to you. You may choose to include sports, physical fitness and health among your priorities; or playing the guitar or the clarinet. Your priority may simply be to create further harmony in your life, or to explore your spiritual side. Your list should reflect a balance. It shouldn't be top-heavy with sports or hobby priorities, just as it shouldn't be top-heavy with school, work and career priorities. The list should be flexible, so that you can add to it, expand, shrink or bend it, but with this list and your mission statement, you should be well on your way to focusing on the type of journey you wish to make. This brings us to the next point. Focus.

There is no use collecting bits of paper with useful lists if you don't do anything with them. Let's take the case of Liz.

Liz wanted to learn how to play the guitar, so she bought a guitar and some 'how to play' books; she even went to some concerts to see guitarists in action. She then bought some more sheet music. She bought a new guitar case. Liz collected all the paraphernalia connected with playing a guitar but left out one ingredient. She never actually got around to learning how to play.

How many people do you know who are busy planning rather than doing? Are you a planner or a doer? It's important not to spend too much valuable time overplanning. It's concerning to see people who are forever drawing up lists, neatly ruling up timetables and arranging their desk. Remember, the goal isn't in the planning, it's in the doing. The plan is a means to an end, not an end in itself. Focus on your direction. The destination is important, but so is the journey. You have to realise that everything you do will build layer upon layer into an exciting and rewarding life. You may not feel you are getting closer to your goals, but you are, every day. Progress may be slow, but its importance to you is what counts. A small acorn doesn't look like much, but it's the start of a gigantic oak tree. It's also important to examine your progress regularly. Examine the setbacks, and be honest with yourself; be gentle with yourself, but remain firmly focused on the issue at hand.

As we keep saying, you need to start somewhere, and you already have. With a little forward planning you have created your own map. You have sorted your priorities and you have your focus. Now, to really make things work you'll need to add a few more ingredients into the mixture, especially discipline, determination and persistence. Read on.

27
Discipline, determination and persistence (DDP)

These three items form the cornerstone of any endeavour, whether it's climbing Mount Everest, starting a new business, learning a musical instrument or building a tree-house. Without 'DDP' it is possible to start something ... but what about finishing it? That's another matter. Let's look at each one in turn, then see how they interlock.

Discipline This is the ability to begin and follow something through to the end, without distraction. It's the ability to 'get the job done'. Discipline makes you turn the TV off so that you can finish that assignment. Discipline tells you to leave for work earlier than usual to get the report finished (and stay back late if it isn't). Discipline also keeps you from messing around with drugs, or over-indulging in alcohol. Discipline can allow you to follow your religious beliefs, keeps you training at the gym, and gets you on your bike on cold winter mornings. Discipline is the rocket-fuel that propels you along, dragging you away from short-term thrills in exchange for long-term benefits.

Discipline, determination and persistence

Determination Again, you can have all the discipline in the world, but it won't help unless you have the determination to see it through. Determination requires a clear goal to strive for and the willpower to head relentlessly towards it. If discipline is the rocket-fuel, then determination is the engine, the driving force. Discipline will get you to the gym; determination will make sure you do the training. Determination will focus your attention on the goal and keep you heading in the right direction. Discipline will get you to your desk at 8.00 am, but real determination will see that the job is finished. You have to 'want' to do something, not just 'like' to do it. Would you like to be a tennis pro, or do you want to be a tennis pro? There is a difference. Sometimes, sheer determination can win through when the discipline has been exhausted. Climbing a mountain requires discipline, but succeeding against all odds—bad weather, equipment failure, hunger, thirst—requires unswerving determination.

Persistence Some people confuse determination with persistence. You can be determined to do something, but if you fail, and give up, then you lack persistence. Persistence is what kept Thomas Edison going through his experiments, most of which failed. Persistence keeps you going in the face of opposition and difficulties. Persistence kept Columbus going, until he discovered land. His crew thought he was wrong, but Columbus persisted. Persistence will keep that wheel turning, even when people say it's not worth it, and others have long given up. Persistence is also about trial and error. You fall over, get up and try again. It's like learning to ride a bike. If everybody who fell off their bike first time around never tried again, there'd be very few bikes on the road. You just have to watch a baby learning to walk to see persistence (and determination) in action: they don't give up, no matter what. Persistence can triumph over

DISCIPLINE, DETERMINATION AND PERSISTENCE

intelligence, qualifications and other labels. Naturally, it's also important to know when to stop, and when it's time to try a different approach. That's called exercising judgement.

Some people say that genius is 1% inspiration and 99% perspiration. Well, that perspiration is DDP. Once you have decided to follow a certain course of action, to do something, to be something, then the focus of your desires and passions will help you to keep at it like a terrier. You won't want to let go until the deed is done. Why do so many people fail at things they try? Courses half-finished, careers half-finished, half-hearted attempts at sports, music and hobbies? Why? They lacked not only the real passion to achieve but also the DDP to see it through. They obviously didn't want these things badly enough.

> Developing DDP is about discovering a passion; something that can start a fire deep within you.

Discipline is also training. It involves the ability to do boring, tiring or repetitive tasks until discipline becomes part of you. Once you have mastered that discipline, determination and persistence keep you moving forward. Discipline is at the core of every athlete, every musician and a part of anyone who wants to rise above mediocrity in their chosen endeavour, be it sport, career or hobby.

Developing DDP is about discovering a passion; something that can start a fire deep within you. It doesn't just happen. You must want something badly enough. You must want to change something badly enough. You must want to excel at something badly enough. DDP seems to follow as a natural consequence. It grows in a hot-house environment where your passion is strong enough.

But DDP may still not be enough to get you through to the end. A couple of other elements need to be added to the

Discipline, Determination and Persistence

formula. The first element is a touch of creativity. Creativity will take your endeavour from the mundane to the marvellous. Creativity, as part of DDP, can let you explore undreamed-of alternatives. It will allow you to look at your situation from a fresh perspective.

The other element to add to our potent mixture is a healthy dose of clear thinking. Clear thinking will allow you to critically evaluate your choices. What's the upside of your decision? What's the downside? You need to be able to weigh up the pros and cons without rushing into something based simply on a gut reaction, then realising all too late that it was the wrong move.

Eve was starting to get fed up with her job. At the age of twenty-five she had been working for a few years with a large corporation and felt it was time to move on. If she only relied on DDP, she would have resigned within days and be gone, without thinking any further. Fortunately, Eve planned her 'escape'. She thought about what she really wanted to do, and thought creatively about all her options. The process for Eve was quite simple. She sat down one night at home with a large sheet of butchers' paper. She wrote down her options—as many as she could think of—and the pros and cons of each option. She then made a short list of options to which she could genuinely apply her DDP. It turned out that Eve's preferred option did not involve resigning at all. The sort of work she wanted to do was available within another division of the same company. It would mean relocating to another state, but she saw that as part of the adventure. She spoke to her supervisor, who agreed with the move, though it would not happen for six months, so Eve commenced a training program which would see her take on new responsibilities with ease. It was work that she would enjoy and she knew that 'Monday-itis' would become a thing of the past. The DDP worked for Eve, as did the added dose of creativity and clear thinking. She

Discipline, Determination and Persistence

didn't rush into anything. She sat back and evaluated her situation and she hasn't looked back since.

Sure, certain circumstances can prevent you from following through, but many people lack staying power once a decision is made. Most inventions, from cars to computers, as well as discoveries in medicine and sporting triumphs, are the result of DDP in men and women who weren't quitters. Again, the choice is yours. Are you a quitter or can you follow through?

28
Attention to detail
nothing works without it

All the good ideas and intentions in the world won't amount to anything if the details aren't followed through. It's very true that it's 'the little things that count'. The little nuts and bolts that hold engines together; the tiny processors and capacitors that keep computers running; the commas and full stops on this page that help the words flow smoothly.

Some of us claim to be 'big picture' people; that is, we like to take an overview of a situation and not pay too much attention to the nitty-gritty details. Others are 'details' people who sweat over the most minute details, often at the expense of the 'big picture'. Neither of these extremes will get us too far. We need to strike a healthy balance between focusing on details at the expense of all else and keeping in sight the overall idea, or project.

Sam is a 'big-picture' kind of guy. Mainly because Sam is a big guy, he could be a bouncer, or a footballer or a wrestler, except he likes to keep to himself. Sam was fixing his car one day. He liked to tinker and fiddle with it on weekends. He decided to pull bits of it apart, clean the engine and

ATTENTION TO DETAIL

re-assemble it. After about three hours the job was finished, except that Sam had a number of nuts and bolts left over. Being a 'big-picture' type of person, he might have considered his job done. He had, after all, put his engine back together. But he realised that minor details could compromise his safety. He had to start all over again, because he had to figure out where those bolts, nuts and screws belonged. Sam could see both the 'big picture' and the details.

Morris is just the opposite. He is 'Mr Detail'. This suits him because he's a little detailed sort of guy. His favourite hobby is building model aeroplanes and model cars. He can sit for hours gluing and assembling the tiniest of components. One day Morris was at work (he's an accountant and loves all those columns of figures and spreadsheets) putting together a presentation for a prospective new client. All the figures were checked and everything looked okay but Morris had lost the perspective of the overall job.

> To put it as clearly as possible, detail can make or break you.

He got so carried away with the figures that he failed to notice he had the client's name wrong on the title page and had left out a page covering the company's trading history. Morris had invested so much time in his precious figures that he lost sight of the overall purpose of the presentation. His eye for detail was too narrow. Morris still can't understand why they didn't get the business.

To put it as clearly as possible, detail can make or break you. You may look great in a new outfit, but scuffed shoes or dandruff on your shoulders can speak volumes about the sort of person you are. If the essay or report you've written reads quite well but is creased and dog-eared, or has spelling errors, it lets the whole project down.

So, how do you develop that eye for detail, without losing the plot of the big picture? First of all, you need to have a very clear sense of what the overall project, job, assignment or whatever, is about and what your goal is. Once you know what you are trying to 'build', create or learn, you can break the whole down into manageable components and concentrate on them. There's no point building fantastic and accurate brick-work if you don't know whether you are building a wall or a bridge. The detail may be fine, but the end result could be a bit of a problem. By all means focus on the brick-work, but keep absolutely clear in your mind what you are building in the first place. To change the metaphor, it's like looking at an aerial photograph of a city, and having a detailed road map. You see the total picture but you also know where you're going.

You are a living, breathing example of a lot of minute detail creating a whole that is truly remarkable. Yet if any of those details are wrong or missing, you would be a less than perfect human being.

Just look at the detail in one of Nature's most wondrous creations—you. Look at your hands, look at the pattern of your skin, look at your face, the intricate detail in your eye. You are a living, breathing example of a lot of minute detail creating a whole that is truly remarkable. Yet if any of those details are wrong or missing, you would be a less than perfect human being.

When you finish something like an assignment, a report, a painting or a model, take a long hard look at it, and check all the details. How can the details be improved? How can the overall item or presentation be improved? Is there anything you have left out? Is the balance right? Give

ATTENTION TO DETAIL

somebody the work to look at; a fresh point of view can often help. Constant practice will train you to be good at this. It is part of the discipline we talked about in chapter 27.

Paying attention to detail will build the biggest ships, the most powerful computers, or the smallest toys and the most compact circuit boards. Like a zoom camera we can zoom in and out of a project and see how the detail works in a broader context. Balancing the two is a skill which will come with time, intuition, practice and constant thought.

29

Procrastination
I'll tell you what it means tomorrow

There are a lot of words that start with 'pro'. There's professional, promotion, progress, prodigy, pro-active, production and so on. They are all positive terms. Procrastination is just the opposite. It's a negative term. It means 'Never do today what you can put off until tomorrow'. It means stall, delay, give it a miss. We have all been guilty of this at some stage. We can procrastinate about all sorts of things, from not taking out the garbage to delaying doing homework, to avoiding dealing with or confronting problems or opportunities at work. Procrastination knows no bounds. Often procrastination goes with a lack of self-confidence or sometimes with apathy, the 'couldn't care less', 'couldn't be bothered' syndrome. If you don't care about something, it's easy to stall and put it off. In order to overcome procrastination it's important to understand the source of it, what caused it to exist in the first place, and the attitudes that are keeping it alive.

Let's take a closer look at some of the causes of procrastination. We may then be a little closer to overcoming it. We delay doing things for a whole variety of reasons. Here's a list of what could be called 'procrastination triggers':

PROCRASTINATION

Too boring	Too confronting
Too hard	Too tedious
Too dirty	Too silly
Too complex	Too shy
Too time-consuming	Too embarrassing

If a given situation involves any (or all) of these points then procrastination is a likely outcome. We are generally very good at rationalising our way out of doing something; we are all experts at that. It is one of the things that separates us from the animal world. Animals can't rationalise; they just get on with it. Lions don't think, 'I'm hungry, but I can't be bothered hunting today ... I'll try again tomorrow.' They just do it.

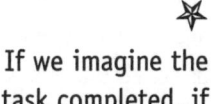

> If we imagine the task completed, if we can imagine how we'd feel when it's all over, then actually doing it may become a lot simpler.

We often delay doing things because, when faced with the enormity or the complexity of the task, we'd rather go out, or watch TV, or arrange our papers, and think that it will be easier tomorrow. But it never is. We simply run away from addressing the task, and hope it will go away. We would rather not deal with it at the moment. Why?

When we procrastinate we are probably obsessed by the task, not the outcome. We tend to be focused on the short term, the drudgery, the difficulty or whatever. But if we shift our thinking and our focus on the completed task, then a whole new world can open to us. If we imagine the task completed, if we can imagine how we'd feel when it's all over, then actually doing it may become a lot simpler. Our motivation is now, 'Why delay the feeling of success any longer?', or 'Why put off the feeling of relief ... let's do it now!'

PROCRASTINATION

Let me tell you about Harry. He is a world authority on avoidance behaviour. You probably know plenty of 'Harrys' at work, school or college. Perhaps you might even see yourself in this description.

Whenever he had a task to do Harry would immediately snap into 'avoidance mode'. He would sharpen pencils, he would tidy his desk, or call some people on the phone, then grab a cup of coffee and perhaps stroll around 'thinking'. Sometimes he'd even write a list of all the things he had to do. There's an important point here. It's okay to write lists of what you have to do, as long as you follow through. Harry just wrote lists and made impressive-looking plans. Instead of actually doing a task, he'd just plan to do it. He was a classic 'gonna'. 'I'm gonna do it soon.' 'I'm gonna do it tomorrow.' 'I'm gonna be a success one day.' Don't be like Harry. Take control. Get the job done or get the homework done. It doesn't matter what it is, just do it, get it out of the way and move on.

Like a lot of behaviour discussed in this book, procrastination is a reflection of your state of mind. If your attitude is good, then procrastination becomes a thing of the past because you will have acquired the discipline to follow through and get the job done. How often have you thought 'I'll do it this afternoon ... ' and then some friends drop over? You think, 'That's okay, I'll do it tonight!' Your friends stay for a pizza and a video. Your day has gone and an opportunity has been missed. You feel guilty and cheated. 'If only I had started it earlier ... ' Instead of working when you had the chance, and finishing the job, you ignored it. Discipline yourself to do the task when it's there, not in an hour, or tonight ... but right now! Focus on how good you'll feel when it's over.

One other important thing to keep in mind. You will often find that once you begin a task it's neither as difficult as you

PROCRASTINATION

expected nor does it take as long as you originally thought it would. Indeed, it might even be more enjoyable than you envisaged. A task commenced is a task on the way to being completed. Sometimes it's a matter of gritting

> A task commenced is a task on the way to being completed.

your teeth and starting the job. If you feel the task is rather daunting or complex, break it down into components, small pieces that you can easily digest and which help to build your confidence along the way. There's no point in tackling a project and thinking you'll hit a 'home run' first up. Give yourself time, be patient and allow yourself the right to make mistakes and learn from them. Review what you have done, reward yourself for progress and don't give up. Remember DDP (Discipline, Determination, Persistence)!

On a personal note, we didn't feel daunted by the task of writing a whole book. We looked at it as a series of individual chapters that would eventually build into this book. There's an old Chinese saying: 'A journey of a thousand miles begins with a single step.' Go on. Take that step. Stop procrastinating and get working on that attitude shift ... right now.

30
The problems of problem-solving

HOW we solve problems is often a reflection of the type of person we are. If we are the type of person who likes to tackle life head-on, then that's how we are likely to approach problem-solving. If we are the type of person who feels easily threatened and shaken, then our approach to problem-solving is likely to be quite timid.

There is no simple, one-step, just-add-water-and-mix guide to problem-solving, because every problem is different. What you may perceive to be a problem, someone else may see as a mere hassle, and as we saw in chapter 11, some problems can also be an opportunity in disguise. However, there are a few basic principles that can be applied to most problems.

We all know people who make a major drama out of simply going shopping for groceries, or who think a minor cold is a real problem that they have to grapple with. The first step is to gain a perspective on the problem. Is it actually a problem, a minor set back, a slight nuisance, or is it a full-blown crisis? Once we decide on our perspective, we can begin to focus on solving it. What we then do is not ignore the problem, but work out how to tackle it, calmly

The Problems of Problem-Solving

and clearly. Don't bury your head in the sand and hope it will go away and sort itself out. Tackle it head-on; once you start to tackle a problem, you are on your way to solving it. By putting off tackling the problem, you put off arriving at a solution. The longer you put it off, the further the solution may slide out of your grasp, and the situation deteriorate.

> Being able to come up with some creative and viable alternatives when something goes off the rails is a skill which can be learnt.

Next you have to know whether or not you can do anything about solving the problem. Certain things cannot be changed. For example, you are all packed and ready to go for a drive; suddenly the weather changes and it starts to rain. You can't change the weather, and there is no use moaning and complaining. Just accept the inevitable. It's going to rain, but that needn't be the end of your adventure. Have a barbecue at home, rent a video, plan an alternative event. Yes, it is a problem that your plans have been messed up, but with some simple problem-solving skills you can find an alternative.

Being able to come up with some creative and viable alternatives when something goes off the rails is a skill which can be learnt. Many people just throw up their hands and give up, which is more a reflection on the person than the magnitude of the problem. Some things can be changed, and some things cannot. Once you know the difference, you can save yourself a lot of stress and heartache. If you have a car smash, you must accept that it has happened, you cannot hope that the metal will uncrumple. The accident has happened: it is a fact, so allow yourself to be upset and angry. Then go on to the next step and do what has to be done to fix it. Problem-solving skills help you to determine

The Problems of Problem-solving

quickly whether or not something has happened. Is it a fact, has something actually happened, or do you merely fear something happening? We move out of 'prevention' mode and into 'cure' or 'solution' mode. Some of us keep going over past events again and again, like watching a replay of an old movie. We replay the events, as if the act of 'viewing' them again can alter the outcome. But it's all 'spilt milk'; it has happened, so it's important to move on to the next phase, whatever that may be, in relation to the problem.

Some problems do call for a more creative approach. Take the legendary case of Alexander the Great. He heard that in a certain town there was a huge, complex knot, that once belonged to Gordius, king of Phrygia. The legend stated that whoever could untie the knot would rule Asia. Many had tried and failed before Alexander arrived. He was told it was difficult, some said impossible, others suggested that he shouldn't go there at all. Alexander arrived and saw the huge knot, walked around it a couple of times, had a good long hard look at it, then took his long, sharp sword and sliced through the knot with one well-aimed stroke. The knot collapsed in front of him. Not long after that event, Alexander the Great became ruler of Asia. Alexander didn't let past preconceptions or assumptions cloud his thinking. Nobody actually told him that he couldn't slice through the knot, he just did it. He didn't accept the traditional way of looking at the problem. Today, 'cutting the Gordian knot' has come to mean solving a difficult problem.

Here's a fun way of discovering how many of your friends rely a little too heavily on assumptions. Get a few of them to line up in a corridor or at the end of a room. Give each one a sheet of paper, and allow five minutes for them to make a projectile. The one that travels the furthest wins. You're likely to see some quite frantic activity, and the most extraordinary

The problems of problem-solving

paper planes will take shape. When everyone has thrown their projectiles, take your sheet of paper, screw it up into a ball and just throw it. You're bound to win. Everybody else will complain and say that it's unfair, and that you 'cheated'. You then say to them that you did not ask them to make a paper plane. You asked them to make a 'projectile'; the winner was the one whose projectile 'travelled' the furthest, the word 'fly' was never mentioned. This is an excellent example of how assumptions and preconceptions can cloud our thinking.

Day in and day out we approach problems the same old way, as if our thinking is in a rut. You know what they say when you 'assume' something? You make an 'ass' out of 'u' and 'me'. We often assume all sorts of things, and when something goes wrong we tend to start our explanation with 'But I assumed ... ' Who asked you to assume or guess an answer?

Always try to look at problems from a fresh point of view. Without that approach, all sorts of inventions would never have happened. Take the invention of the helicopter, for example. Birds have wings; therefore if you want to fly you need to have some sort of machine with wings just like a bird's. But the helicopter broke through that assumption. They fly without bird-like wings, and are far more versatile than any plane.

Try to look at problems from different perspectives. For example, if you are having a problem with a friend, colleague, or neighbour, try looking at the same problem from the other person's point of view. You may be surprised how that shift in perspective can help solve the problem. You may need to negotiate your way out of a problem; this can involve a little give and take, but again there doesn't have to be only one correct outcome. You should allow for the possibility of a number of solutions.

The problems of problem-solving

Decision-making also needs to be handled carefully. If possible, make sure you have all the facts at hand; but also be prepared to make decisions quickly when you don't have time to gather all the facts. In an emergency, we need to act and think fast, but in normal circumstances decision-making should be done carefully. Does the decision involve signing a contract? Is it a decision about a major purchase? Is it a decision about starting or ending a relationship? Just think clearly, and move slowly, and be very aware of the consequences of your decision. Remember, it's your choice, so take the responsibility. The last thing you want to be saying to yourself is 'I should've thought of that ... ' or 'But I assumed that ... '

A lot of things that we worry and panic about never happen. When we worry about what might happen, we experience the effects of the problem as if it had actually happened. For example, you may leave home in the morning, unsure if you actually closed or locked the front door. All day long, you are filled with fear and wild imaginings about burglars walking in and out of your house. You are even too nervous to eat lunch. Remember, at this stage the fear is about an imagined event. You have no proof that anything has actually happened. You finally rush home, biting your nails, sweat pouring off you, and guess what: the door is locked and had been all along. Then you feel silly because you worried about this 'problem' all day. The lesson is simple. React to a fact, not some imagined consequence. Just because you think something has happened, or might happen, doesn't mean it will. Put your reaction on hold until you have the facts. Don't put yourself through hell because of an over-active imagination. To solve a problem, first make sure it *is* a problem.

31
Does your 'dream gauge' show 'full' or 'empty'?

Is it possible ever to run out of dreams? Not the dreams we dream at night, but the dreams that drive us forward. Our 'wish list', all those sentences that start with 'Wouldn't it be nice if'.

Do we have some kind of 'dream gauge' within us that at a certain age shows full to the brim, but as we get older gradually empties? It is a tragedy that many people are running on 'empty' and they don't even realise it, yet they let the world know about it in all sorts of other ways.

Have you ever returned to a place that held treasured memories for you, only to find that once you arrived it wasn't the same? Sure, you've changed, maybe the place has changed too, but perhaps what made it so special in the first place were the dreams you had back then, the future that you held in the palm of your hand. If you return to such a place unfulfilled, or devoid of dreams, then you won't rekindle anything; you're likely to feel self-pity and empty nostalgia for what could have been.

DOES YOUR 'DREAM GAUGE' SHOW 'FULL' OR 'EMPTY'?

Take Wendy for example. She went on holidays as a nineteen-year-old to a seaside resort. She remembered that holiday fondly because she was just about to start tertiary studies and knew that she was going overseas after her degree was finished. It was a great holiday, full of anticipation and joy. Ten years later she returned to the same beach. This time her family was with her, her husband and two-year-old son. How did she feel? Great. She walked along the same beaches and the same pier and relived in a very positive way her last visit. Now she is about to re-enter the workforce. Her old boss wants her back, she has a wonderful family, and all those dreams did come true. She did it. She lived her dreams. Returning to that beach filled her with a warm sense of accomplishment; she also knew the best was yet to come. It's unlikely her dream gauge will ever show 'empty'.

When we are younger we tend to want a lot of material things. A nice car, trendy clothes, a CD player with the works, overseas holidays ... in fact, everything. That's okay, there's nothing wrong with that. It's all part of growing up. These dreams are so often the fuel that propels us forward. The dreams motivate us to work, earn money, do well and so on. We eventually do get the right car, the great stereo system and the overseas trip. But then what? We've climbed that mountain and got bored with the view. Our dreams, like any fuel, need constant replenishing. They need topping up.

> Our dreams, like any fuel, need constant replenishing. They need topping up.

Many people reach middle age with their dream gauge low-fuel-warning light permanently on and perilously close to showing empty. Dreams have given way to cynicism, negativism and just plain survival. There is little left that is worth striving for. The pattern has been established and the fear of change keeps the dream gauge showing 'low'. Paying

DOES YOUR 'DREAM GAUGE' SHOW 'FULL' OR 'EMPTY'?

the mortgage, getting through the traffic and just getting by are now the priorities. Where have all the dreams gone?

Sure, by this stage of their lives some people have the means to buy whatever they want, but somehow life has become a little too easy, a little too comfortable. Their dreams need to take on a different dimension. Just acquiring possessions can become an empty, competitive task. The excitement of buying is in the anticipation, not the acquiring. To refill the dream tank we need imagination, goals, plans, actions. We need to understand that dreams can include a rich emotional life as well as goals in the external world. Fulfilling dreams is a rare pleasure that few are lucky enough to experience. But it's important to keep the dream tank full and not to take a defeatist approach. Striving is a part of the dream, and to keep reaching for dreams is part of what life is about. Without dreams, great or small, what is there to strive for?

> Without dreams, great or small, what is there to strive for?

Your goals may include doing better at school or work, getting a promotion or even changing a career altogether, writing that book or play, learning to dance or play the piano. Whatever it is, keep the dream tank full and set yourself goals and achievable targets.

By keeping your dream gauge showing 'full', you will be able to integrate important aspects of your life to reflect how you think and plan, and what adventures you are prepared to tackle. Your dreams won't simply be about acquiring, but will also be about 'doing' and 'being'. They will reflect your inner life. After all, where else could your dreams come from?

Your goals may not be lofty, or make you rich and famous, but with a full tank of dreams you'll be able to travel further.

32
The patience perspective

Rush, rush, rush. Everybody wants everything right now, this moment. You see something in a shop: you want it now. You see someone you think you like: you want to fall in love straight away. You develop a hobby or a career goal, and you want to be at the pinnacle now. Even tomorrow is too late ... Whatever happened to patience? Whatever happened to nurturing ideas and relationships, carefully growing, attending to career plans and enjoying life along the way?

Events in the world around us seem to be accelerating at a phenomenal speed. Mass media and technology have created instant demand and equally instant gratification. Before fax machines, people were happy to wait for the mail to deliver the information. The response would be similarly slow. Now, a fax spews out of a machine and demands to be read and dealt with immediately. The time between thought and action is now very short indeed. Our daily lives are also crowded with events, personal, work-related or scholastic. There's no time to stop and think. Patience seems to be a remnant of a bygone era, long fossilised, as old as a dinosaur bone. In many ways we have become servants of the technology. It seems that technology has robbed us of the ability to create the patience perspective.

THE PATIENCE PERSPECTIVE

You will find some aspects of your life are like a garden. They need plenty of care and planning, as well as nourishment. You can't rush the growth of a plant or a tree. Everything happens in its own sweet time and pace. You can't get plums before the blossoms appear, and that doesn't happen until spring. Nature has its own pattern, and its own patience perspective.

> ✵
> You have the choice to hold up an imaginary 'stop' sign and take the time to think, re-evaluate and quietly form an opinion.

Some things in your life can't be rushed or accelerated either. They have their own in-built rhythm or pattern.

Choices—we come back to choices all the time. You have the choice to hold up an imaginary 'stop' sign and take the time to think, re-evaluate and quietly form an opinion about the subject at hand. Get into the habit of forming a special retreat or 'quiet room' in your mind. Shut out the noise, the confusion and chatter of the world around you. In this quiet oasis you are free to contemplate, and re-assess your situation. We often talk about 'running out of patience' (sounds a bit like a flat battery doesn't it?). In your quiet room, you can recharge this valuable and precious resource. You need never run out of it again.

What exactly does patience mean, and what can it do for you? It can be defined as a tolerant and even-tempered perseverance habit. It's a skill that you develop to give yourself the breathing space you require. Let's say someone offers you a job. You currently have a job so there is no pressure on you to take it. When you have the patience perspective, you can take the time to think. You don't have to rush in and say 'yes'. Neither do you have to hang up the phone with an abrupt 'no'. Patience will allow you to persevere in the evaluation of the situation. You can work

The Patience Perspective

out what your options are. What are the advantages or disadvantages of this offer? Do you need to negotiate the terms of the offer? If you are patient and give yourself a little breathing space, you can make a more informed decision because your thinking hasn't been unduly hampered by immediate reactions.

Patience comes into play in all areas of our lives. Patience is important in our relationships. Your partner is given room to grow and think. Decisions aren't rushed: the pressure is turned right down. Too many couples, for example, get married and want everything straight away. They want a house, a car or two, furniture, the lot. If they applied the patience perspective they would realise that there doesn't have to be a rush to accumulate wealth, material possessions, knowledge, or insight. Patience can act as an important check and balance system in your life. The habit of perseverance goes well with judgement and determination and keeps us from rushing into situations that could be potentially harmful.

Similarly, in our relationships with our children and other young people, we need to be patient so that they learn and acquire confidence and self-esteem along the way.

Tim was twenty-two years old and desperate to learn how to play the piano. During his first year of lessons, he changed piano teachers three times. He felt he was not learning fast enough. Tim didn't realise that he was the problem, not the teacher. After two years Tim stopped learning. He gave up in disgust. He always called his teachers 'hopeless nerds'. All they wanted him to do was practise. All he wanted to do was play. Tim lacked the patience to persevere, to learn to crawl before he walked. By quitting, he denied himself the pleasures of steadily learning and seeing that skill gradually develop. Perhaps some day Tim will return to the piano with a different perspective, the patience perspective.

THE PATIENCE PERSPECTIVE

The second half of the term we've been using is 'perspective' and that's exactly what you need. You need to widen your vision to imagine what will happen in the future. For a moment you need to be able to 'fast-forward' events to gain a broader perspective: get into the habit of 'fast-forwarding'—it's a very useful tool. We all know people who are always in a hurry, dashing here and there. In traffic they speed ahead of everybody else; they know all the shortcuts and zig-zag through side streets ... and why? So they can get somewhere just a few minutes faster than you. Big deal. If you put your imagination in 'fast-forward' mode you'll work out whether or not it's worth going to all that trouble.

> Some things in life can't be changed but your response and attitude can.

Some people are happy to sit at the lights and take the view that they'll arrive whenever they arrive. They are patient and 'go with the flow'. Those who zip through traffic should realise that their behaviour will change little and may add to their already high stress levels. So what if they save five minutes? At least if you take your time you know you won't have an accident, or cause one either. Keep a perspective on your behaviour. 'Fast-forward' to the consequences and you'll find that you may as well be patient. Some things in life can't be changed but your response and attitude can.

It's very easy to be seduced into a headlong rush down a career path, or a rush to acquire all sorts of material possessions, accolades, awards and qualifications. But in this rush we tend to lose a lot as well. A certain amount of 'quality of life' is sacrificed. Family life is sacrificed on the altar of career and money. There is nothing wrong with being focused on your goal, but it must be with a sense of balance that takes into account the journey along the way. If

The patience perspective

you take a long-term view, and use the patience perspective as a way of again fast-forwarding into the future, you might realise that there may not be such a need for rushing and being in a hurry. By being a little more patient, you'll see a lot of things that others miss and a lot of elements in your life, especially your family and relationships, can be enjoyed to their maximum potential.

Alan is seventy-eight years old and quite sprightly for his age. Looking back on his life in 'rewind' mode, he now wonders why he was always in a hurry. He was in a hurry for his career to move forward. He was in a hurry to see his family grow up. He was in a hurry, full stop. Now, looking back, he's sad. He realises that many of those moments are now lost to him forever, because he lacked the patience to enjoy each stage of growth and change and to accept that things take their time. Alan isn't sure if it was all worth it. His children are now grown up and lead their own lives in other parts of the country. He lives in a small house with his wife, Sophie. He remembers that he didn't have much patience with his children. They were always making 'mistakes', and not doing the right thing. Besides, Alan was busy with his career, too busy roaring up the ladder of success to take much notice of family or friends. Now, from the perspective of someone who has been through it all, Alan just isn't sure if it was worth the effort and the stress. Sure, he provided well for his family: good schools, holidays, clothes, but some of the really important things, the spiritual and emotional nourishment, weren't there.

Alan misses the little things most of all. He often thinks about a play his daughter Angela was in when she was six (over forty years ago). He couldn't attend because he had an 'important' business meeting. Forty years later he can't remember what that meeting was about, but he can still remember Angela's tearful face when he told her that he couldn't make it to the play. If only Alan

THE PATIENCE PERSPECTIVE

had developed the perspective to sort out his priorities, or had been a little more flexible. Today, Alan has all the time in the world, but somehow now it is too late.

Finally, patience should not be an excuse to avoid making decisions, or to shirk responsibility. Keep things in balance. Sometimes it's important to react quickly. At other times, it's equally appropriate to put the brakes on, take it easy ... then act. The patience perspective, blended with other life skills, can add some important balance to your life.

33
It's about time

Used wisely, time is a friend. When frittered away, it's an enemy. You don't have to wear a watch to be aware of time. Nor do you need to be a slave to time by constantly being reminded of what the time is. Most of us are surrounded by clocks, in our homes, in the car, at work. In a meeting we don't need to keep looking at a watch: the meeting will finish when the agenda is completed. If it is important enough for us to be there, we should be focusing on the meeting; not on what time it is.

If we are rushing to another appointment, we can ask the time. If we are at a play, for example, we don't need to look at a watch. If we are bored, we walk out, otherwise the play will take its course. It will finish when it finishes, no matter how often we look at our watches.

Time can be used wisely, or it can be squandered. If you know that you have a deadline to meet, take responsibility for your actions, and use the available time to complete the task (take another look at chapter 29 on procrastination). Don't stall and think you'll do it later; invariably something else will come up. Time is like any other precious finite resource.

If you have a hobby, say, making clothes—or anything else that fascinates you—then you'll notice that time simply flies by. The last thing you're likely to do is look at your watch.

It's about time

The task at hand has totally absorbed you. At the outset you don't say 'I'll spend an hour on this jacket then quit'. You simply keep working away. You will find that you don't need to keep looking at a watch. You get used to knowing that it's about 3.15, or just after 6.00, or almost 5.00. Perhaps wearing a watch and constantly checking the time has become more of a habit than a necessity. Try leaving the watch at home and enjoy the freedom.

> Don't reach the age of fifty, and be filled with regrets about what you should have done, or almost did. Use time now to do those things.

As you get older, you become aware that time seems to be accelerating. When you are ten years old, summer seems to last forever. When you are thirty years old, it just flies by. Don't reach the age of fifty, and be filled with regrets about what you should have done, or almost did. Use time now to do those things. And if you are fifty, don't use your age as an excuse . . .

Take control. Do those things you've been putting off. Most people who complain that they don't have time really mean that they don't have the passion commitment, or DDP. They have time to watch TV at night, they have time to go to the pub, or time to go to the football, of course. It's okay to do these things. But allocate some time to invest in yourself, in your future, in your family, and your friends. This could simply mean taking the time to go for a picnic with your family. Take the time to enrol in a part-time or evening course; take the time to learn a sport. Take the time to balance your life, and re-examine priorities. Isn't it amazing that if there is something you really want to do, or would enjoy, there's always plenty of time, but if the going gets a little tough . . . no time . . . and no commitment. Remember, even though time is not always on your side, you can

It's about time

organise your time in a way that reduces stress, tension, wastage and, ultimately, regrets.

Let's look at Reg. He works in a large public company. His day is totally driven by time. Every morning he catches the 8.03 from his station to make it into town on time. At exactly 8.49 he's walking through the front doors. Morning tea is at 10.00. Lunch is strictly 1–2.00 pm. Afternoon tea is at 3.00 and he clocks off at 5.15. Precisely. Reg knows what he should be doing, and where he should be because of what time it is.

We understand that the world works in a particular way; that one has to arrive at work or school at a particular time and leave at a particular time. Structures in our lives can work well, but there has to be flexibility and an understanding of the reason for the structures. In earthquake zones, for example, buildings must be constructed in such a way that they give and move during a 'quake. Rigid, inflexible buildings just collapse. The structures in our lives have to have some 'give' in them too. Imagine for a moment that Reg breaks his routine. He discovers that with flexitime he can start later, and stay longer. He can catch a later train. Time suddenly stops being such a harsh taskmaster and becomes a friend. Reg feels less regimented. He has more freedom to work when he wants to and spend time on other activities important to him.

It's okay to stick to a rigid timetable if you are happy with what inflexibility delivers. It's not okay if your whole life is driven by the timetable, and limits your choices. Sometimes we have rigid timetables because it's part of the system we are in. At school there are timetables for classes, and the same applies to higher education. We are asking you to accept the spirit of this information rather than to take it too literally. Dental and other appointments have to be kept; deadlines have to be adhered to—otherwise chaos would reign. However, it is important to treat time as an ally, to use it as such, and between those cracks in your schedule you can really make things happen. Don't throw your schedule or timetable away. Just re-examine your approach to time in general.

We are also not necessarily asking you to convince your teachers or colleagues to let you start your day an hour later. What we are saying is that if you feel driven, if you feel that you are on an endless conveyor belt, work out how to slow down the process, or alter it, to give yourself more freedom and choice. If you think you might be more productive doing things a little differently, it's worth discussing. For example, more and more organisations are allowing people to work from home for a portion of the week. With faxes and portable computers, your physical location is becoming less and less important. It's what you do, not necessarily where or when you do it, that counts.

Working from nine to five is beginning to seem more of a relic of the Industrial Age than a symptom of the rapidly accelerating Information Age in which we are now living. Work practices and attitudes are changing, and an aspect of these changes includes a new way of looking at time and how it affects us.

As a way of understanding the process, try monitoring how you use time. Are you a clock watcher? Do you waste time? Do you have time to 'kill'? Do you get bored, and then complain you never have any free time? Examine your daily schedule and see where you can use time more effectively. Can you read during a coffee break? Can you take a brisk walk at lunchtime? Can you get home early and go for a bike ride? Can you get up an hour earlier and read, exercise, learn something or simply meditate? The opportunities to make better use of time are there. We only have to look for them and be committed to following through.

Throughout this third part of the book we have addressed a range of important issues relating to learning, thinking and planning. (Part one covered fundamental issues concerning attitudes, beliefs and values. Part two looked at our complex range of emotions and feelings.) It should be obvious by now that if you want to alter your life as a result of exploring issues raised in this book, you need to devote time and effort. No instant 'fix' or solution will be handed to you on a platter. Use time to discover yourself, like an explorer venturing through an unexplored continent.

Whether time becomes a friend or foe is entirely up to you.

Part 4

Relating and communicating

34
Relating and relationships
putting in and taking out

It really is pretty incredible: human beings can fly to the moon, build the most powerful computers imaginable and yet still seem to have real trouble understanding that most basic and primitive human reality —relationships with other people.

Maybe we should begin by examining what sort of relationships there are and those we desire. We have all been in different kinds of relationships: short-term, long-term, deep, superficial, convenient, work-related, just to mention a few. We tend to expect different things from the various relationships we are in. Similarly, we tend to behave according to the nature of the relationship.

Whilst relationships of convenience or necessity (e.g. working arrangements) may fulfil a variety of our needs, we are likely to derive the greatest amount of personal enrichment from those long-term, constantly evolving relationships where we are prepared to make the greatest emotional investment. These are the relationships where we build deep connections and bonds with those whom we love and care for, not because they can 'do' things for us, but because our relationship is based on mutual trust and affection. The investment in such relationships is not about

> ✯
> From time to time we need to stop and take a break, just to undergo an emotional 'tune-up' to see how our relationships are going.

material returns, but about real emotional responses and the underlying sense of belonging and caring.

It seems, however, that for many people relationships can be a bit like driving an automatic car: just put them into 'S' for 'same as ever' and keep on going—because you've been going for so long you don't know how to stop or change direction. In fact, the steering and gears eventually jam up and rust. If relationships aren't regularly nourished they simply die. It is therefore essential that our important relationships receive regular maintenance checks. From time to time we need to stop and take a break, just to undergo an emotional 'tune-up' to see how our relationships are going. Are we being straight, honest, and up-front? We also need to ascertain whether we are getting what we want from our relationships and whether we are making the appropriate emotional commitment.

We cherish our relationships with those we care for. Things might not always go 'our way', but the underlying bond continues. As it deepens, we end up with greater insight into our own emotional needs and a clearer understanding of the sort of relationships we want and need. The insight into the type of emotional bonds we create with people has enormous implications for every aspect of our lives, underscoring the kinds of relationships we have with our family and friends, and how we treat or interact with our work colleagues.

Contrast a relationship we really value, one with real meaning in our lives, with a relationship full of hidden

Relating and relationships

agendas and plagued with the 'what can I get out of the other person' or 'how many points can I score' syndrome. The latter is a very common game where, although there is some pay-off, there are no real winners. Such relationships are devoid of real caring, trust or honesty and there is no attempt to understand the other person's needs. There is no putting in: simply taking out. The structure of these relationships usually revolves around a power imbalance where the status of one person is compared with that of the other. Such a basis for bonding between two people is likely to cause trouble because the survival of the relationship relies on that structure remaining in place. If there is no deeper emotional bond connecting the two people, and the basis of the relationship changes, there is little left to keep it alive.

It is only once you really start to give the other person the space, time and consideration to be understood and to express themselves, that you begin to explore the relationship in a way previously not thought possible. No longer does fear or anxiety plague it.

However, life rarely goes according to plan. Inevitably there are going to be lots of interesting developments associated with our important relationships. Try to enjoy them, and accept that such developments are inevitable. Of course, when a relationship is built upon real understanding and communication, how much easier it will be to accept one another's shortcomings. Think how different life could be if we really invested ourselves in all our relationships. We could transform not only ourselves, but our world.

Who knows, maybe over time we can even enjoy watching our partner squeeze the toothpaste tube from the middle and accept the towels being folded the 'wrong' way. Just think, if we could give our relationships an opportunity to develop in a more accepting, caring and open way, we might really be able to enjoy them!

35
Dealing with people
it takes all types

Let's face it, as individuals we are all different. It would certainly be a boring and very predictable world if we were all the same. This chapter is about recognising that the world is made up of unique individuals just like you, with likes, dislikes, and an enormous range of feelings, attitudes, beliefs, strengths, weaknesses and preconceptions.

By recognising that the people we deal with are individuals, we can give them the respect, space and consideration that they deserve. We need to be perceptive and intuitive enough to understand the nature of the person we are dealing with, whether they be a colleague, a friend, a boss, a husband or wife or child. We need to be able to pick up clues from the way people act as to how we can best deal with and relate to them. Think of the people you are with at home, at work, school or college, the ones you know well by name. How well do you really know them? What sort of people are they?

> ✴
> Think of the people you are with at home, at work, school or college, the ones you know well by name. How well do you really know them?

Dealing with People

Joe is a salesman, a not-too-successful salesman. He sells insurance, and does well enough to get by. Joe knows his sales-pitch by heart. He knows what to say and when to say it. He thinks he has it all worked out, but the sales keep slipping through his fingers. The more successful agents write twice as much business as Joe. One day, Joe's supervisor, Mal, notices that Joe's sales have been slipping, so Mal suggests that he goes out on a few calls with Joe to see if he can spot what the problem could be. Joe assures Mal that it will probably be a waste of time. The problem has more to do with the economy, perhaps, or people's attitudes towards insurance. Mal isn't a supervisor for nothing. He goes with Joe anyway, just as an observer. What Mal discovered that day would change Joe's life and fortunes for ever. Mal discovered that Joe treated everybody the same way. Sure he was polite and courteous and he knew his products, but he didn't pay attention to his customers. He was like a robot programmed to go house-calling.

Joe is a fairly confident sort of fellow and he didn't see that some of his customers didn't like the full-on big smile and the firm handshake. He didn't see that some customers would have preferred a more down-to-earth, quiet sell, based on information rather than bravado. Joe also broke one crucial rule. He didn't listen. When Mrs Ellison wanted more information because she didn't understand something, Joe just kept ploughing ahead with his routine. He was like an actor going through his paces on stage without noticing that the audience had long since left the theatre. Mal and Joe had some long talks.

Over the next few weeks, Joe started to pay more attention to his customers. If they were slightly quieter, he would adapt his style to suit them. If they were the type who needed facts and figures rather than glib statements, he'd provide that information. By listening to clients, he was able to assess just what sort of person he was dealing with, and he learnt to make a quick assessment within a minute or two of meeting them. Recently, Joe was awarded the Number Two agent's prize in his firm. He had developed his ability to understand and tune into people better, which meant he could deal with them more effectively.

How often have you been cornered at a party by a know-all who talks and talks and talks at you to the point where you can't get a single word in? They seem to ignore your body language, saying that you are bored. They don't pick up the subtle signals we all send out that we would like to terminate the conversation. When you tune into your friends and colleagues on a subtle, non-verbal level you may find that you'll be able to interact in a shorthand but more effective manner. You'll also begin to appreciate more readily that understanding others takes patience and a lot of hard work.

Sometimes we need to adapt our responses to a situation. Most of us do it instinctively. We behave differently with a bank manager or our boss than we do at the gym, or on a night out at the movies. It's equally important to realise that people respond differently to different types. You may not relate well to overly quiet, shy people. Conversely, you may not be able to relate to extroverts, but you still need to be able to understand the other person. We are in no way advocating that you change personality with every encounter. You can't; but you do need to understand and adapt to the environment and the people in it. If you are a university student, for example, and your lecturer is a calm, quiet person, he or she will probably relate to you better in a meeting if you can respect the low-key personality and tune in to that 'frequency'. But that same low-key approach may not suit the more jovial, out-going tutor you see the same day. So again, develop the insight and understanding to adapt to a more casual style and be aware and considerate of the nature of the person you are relating to.

Just as we adapt a driving style to suit changing weather conditions, so at times we need to adapt our responses to suit the environment and the people we deal with. This does not mean compromising honesty or sincerity; nor does it mean trying to change other people's behaviour or judge them in some belligerent way. It does take all types and the sooner you recognise that, the sooner you'll be able to handle situations more effectively and productively. Your relationships will become more positive, rewarding and enriching.

36
Changing others or yourself
which comes first?

Wherever he went, whatever he was doing, whoever he was speaking to, Ian was always giving advice. He couldn't help himself. On whatever subject, there was always the same pontificating about why someone else was wrong. It was virtually impossible to tell Ian anything. He knew everything, he actually believed he had the answer to everything. In fact, Ian knew the whole meaning of life and wasn't afraid to tell everybody!

Usually, when he started on a favourite topic, be it the country's economic woes or what was wrong with the company he worked for, there was no stopping him. He always knew how things could be improved. Even when colleagues criticised him for poor performance, or friends criticised his habits, he never saw any truth in what they said. How could there possibly be anything wrong with him? He was the one who always gave advice. He really believed that he didn't need to change anything. After all, with so much wisdom and knowledge in his head, how could he possibly be the one who needed to change?

CHANGING OTHERS OR YOURSELF?

The problem was that recently Ian had become unbearable to his friends and colleagues. The gratuitous advice and comments simply never ended. One close friend, Uri, became so frustrated and annoyed by Ian's incessant attempts to get him to change his appearance that he stopped seeing him. Other friends too were becoming sick and tired of Ian's endless interference. Before long he was very much on his own. The audience he had so heavily relied on to listen to his advice and make him feel good had all but vanished. Soon there was only himself left to change and that was a prospect he found too daunting to contemplate.

At last Ian started to recognise that something might be wrong but he didn't seem to be able to do much about it. He still didn't see anything wrong with the way he behaved or why he should have to change. He still thought it was always the others who needed changing.

Whether we like to admit it or not, there might be just a touch of Ian in all of us. Most of us like to hold audience and dispense advice when we can. Most of us like to think that we know 'the answer' and want to have the satisfaction of changing the other person, as if that would be an achievement. Perhaps we should consider whether behaviour like Ian's simply reinforces established patterns of reacting or responding to others. Such behaviour will never allow us to develop really close, intimate and meaningful relationships with others. Why? Because we are too busy trying to influence the other person without trying to listen and understand what they are saying. The need to push our own agenda is often uppermost in our minds.

> The true starting point is to learn to change our own attitudes rather than trying to change others.

But what follows if you do 'conquer' the other person by changing them? Where does the relationship go; how does it develop? You may feel like the champion, and the other person may feel defeated. Then what?

The true starting point is to learn to change our own attitudes rather than trying to change others. In the end, all attempts to change other people will be short-term, frustrating and ultimately a failure. Each person must take responsibility for being their own engine of change. No matter how much we may dislike someone's behaviour or mannerisms, we have no right to change them. They might be quite happy being the way they are. For long-term results we must make a genuine commitment to change ourselves. Nobody can do this for us.

In the final analysis, it becomes a choice between whether my courage to change myself is stronger than my desire to continue to control and change others. And there can be a bonus. In bringing about change in yourself, you may help others to reflect on their own lives. Then the greatest of surprises may occur! Far from not having any effect, your own transformation may bring about positive changes to others.

37
Comparing yourself to others
the big trap

This is really a companion chapter to the one on competitiveness (chapter 10). Comparing yourself to others can be a basis of being competitive, and probably also involves a degree of envy. If you want a better car, a better house, a better job, it's so often because you would like to be seen to be doing well. You may even have someone in mind who is a 'competitiveness target'. 'Wait until Jack sees this car ... he'll flip ... it's so much better than his ... '

So many people go through life wishing that they were bigger, smaller, thinner. Wishing that they were as smart as, or smarter than, someone else, or feeling like a failure because they are not as well off as someone else. Of course, it's all relative. Perhaps they think like this because it saves them the trouble of finding out more about themselves. If you find yourself envying others, stop and consider that there may be hundreds, perhaps thousands, of people around the world who would love to swap places with you, in spite of all your 'faults' and all your 'problems'. The truth is that you will always be better off and luckier than a lot of

Comparing Yourself to Others

> ✯ Playing the game of comparisons has no winners, only losers.

other people, even though there will always be people who appear to be better off than you. There are some things in life that you can change and improve; there are other things you can't. The sooner you learn the difference, the sooner you'll have some peace of mind and be free to focus on the things that truly matter in your life and to implement the changes you want. At the same time, the sooner you realise that life is not greener on the other side, the better off you'll be. Focus on your own patch and make it greener.

We are not suggesting here that you grimly accept that this is how things are and how they will always be. You can be your own agent of change. Some things can be changed and some can't. It's a wise person who knows the difference.

Playing the game of comparisons has no winners, only losers. It's important to realise the dangers and shortcomings of defining yourself in relation to others. You don't need to define yourself in relation to your possessions. You don't need to define yourself in relation to the quality or quantity of your friends, or your position at work. Possessions, friends and status fulfil certain needs, but they should not define who we are. So often our comparisons are superficial and transitory. They are about cars, clothes, houses, and other objects. Seldom do we make comparisons like these:

JOHN: I wish I had the same sort of attitudes to life and values that Alex has ...

MANDY: The Andersons seem to have a very stress-free lifestyle. And it has nothing to do with money either ... They're just like that ... How do they do it?

> MIKE: Paul has so much control of his life, his destiny ... whereas I seem just the opposite ... totally out of control ...

Our comparisons reflect our priorities. How many of us envy the Dalai Lama and his harmony in dealing with all his problems? How many of us make comparisons with the some of the great thinkers, artists and philanthropists of this century such as Sigmund Freud, Albert Einstein, Pablo Picasso and Mother Teresa? If we do envy these people, if we do make comparisons, it's because of who they are, or what they have achieved, rather than what they have.

A lot of the trouble with comparisons has to do with the difference between 'having' and 'being'. If we are more interested in having then we are bound to be preoccupied with the pursuit of acquiring more and more. We will always fall into the trap of comparing ourselves with others, and be dissatisfied. If we are interested in what we are and can become, then comparison with others takes on far less significance.

Is there a positive side to making comparisons? Of course there can be. If you gain strength, inspiration and determination from seeing what someone else has achieved, and that goads you into action, the comparison has had a beneficial effect. If there is a sportsperson you admire or a literary hero or someone you look up to, it's helpful to say 'I'm going to be like that person one day ... I know it!', rather than to say 'Why can't I be like them? I'll never amount to anything'. The comparison is the same but the viewpoint is different.

Sometimes comparisons can make us very angry. They may, for example, hold up an image that we feel is unattainable. But if the comparison can make us just angry enough to push us into action, then the outcome may be quite positive.

COMPARING YOURSELF TO OTHERS

Finally, be careful when making comparisons about what others have and what you don't have. Apart from the points covered earlier, you never know the full story behind the other person's perceived success. They may look and act successful, but perhaps the basis is a fortune inherited from a relative. Or perhaps the outward appearances hide huge debts. 'Success' often hides worries and hassles. In fact, you may get a better night's sleep than the person you envy. Who knows, despite all your fears and anxieties, they may even envy *you* ...

38
Peer groups
can you handle the pressure?

Peer group pressure—a familiar term that describes a very subtle mechanism. To an extent we all like to be part of some group. Belonging to a group can give our lives meaning and reinforce values, attitudes and beliefs. Today, one of the most common identifiers to belonging to a young group is to wear a pair of jeans. Faded, torn, patched, whatever, a pair of jeans makes a statement about us. If we turn up to a formal event in jeans, we are making a statement about ourselves. A lot of businesses can be characterised by a certain dress code. If you work in the creative department of an advertising agency, jeans are almost mandatory. If you are an accountant or lawyer, a suit is always expected. If you work in a factory, overalls may be the order of the day. Chances are that you are wearing clothes right now that identify you with a particular group. Even casual clothes speak volumes.

The irony is that whilst teenagers advocate their individuality, they are, at the same time, very susceptible to peer group pressure, which requires a large degree of conformity. There is usually a specific dress code defining the type of jeans, shirt, sweater and sneakers combination. We have to identify with a certain style and the brand name has crept in as a status symbol. It's not enough to wear a particular style of clothing; you now have to wear a particular brand. Without the right logo on the t-shirt you get labelled as some sort of outcast. Non-conformists will be ostracised, but you can form your own group of non-logo wearers—or start a new trend within your existing circle of friends. At the same time you proclaim your individuality and firmly brand yourself as a member of a group.

Peer group pressure, however, goes beyond the clothes you wear. It can define your values and behaviour, in fact your entire lifestyle. If you are part of a peer group called the 'bikies', for example, your entire lifestyle can pretty much be predetermined: the clothes you wear, the friends you have and of course the sort of motorbike you ride. Conformity again, within that group, goes without saying. If you are part of a peer group that belongs to a certain golf or polo club, your common traits would be your socio-economic standing, possibly your choice of suburb, profession and the type of car you drive. The group you are in reflects your attitudes, beliefs and values. You like the sense of belonging, of being part of a team with a lot of shared expectations, with each member reinforcing and 'mirroring' the values of the group.

> If you can accept that as an individual you are unique, it is a lot easier to resist defining yourself through a group.

Being part of a peer group is okay. Our primary peer group, called the human race, can be split into an infinite number of groups and sub-groups using any criteria you like from educational background, religion, height, or whether or not you like pizza. Even so, when you are part of a group or a 'gang' you may sometimes feel that perhaps you don't belong. There may be a conflict between the group's direction and your own values. For example, you may not like the fact that you are the only non-smoker. You may discover that some members of your peer group are involved in illegal activities that cause you conflict. You like the other members of the group, but perhaps in some areas they're going a little too far. In a case like that you need to have the courage to believe in your own value system, to leave the group, and make your own way. In the end, you have a responsibility to act in a way that maintains your own integrity and authenticity, even if it means being rejected by the group.

If you can accept that as an individual you are unique, that there is nobody like you, with your background, beliefs, skills, then it is a lot easier to resist defining yourself through a group. Your security comes from within and is self-generated, rather than coming from an external source. Once you accept this, the need to belong decreases and you are less likely to be 'sucked in' by brand names and logos. Manufacturers rely on peer group pressure to sell the products. The good news is that you don't have to play the game. The group's values can alter as quickly as a particular fashion changes, but if you have a sense of who you are, you can be rock-steady in the face of it all. You don't need to be influenced by passing fads and gimmicks.

Ultimately, the approval of your friends isn't as important to you as your self-esteem. Peer groups can work well if the individuals are allowed to develop, express and assert themselves. They do not need blind conformity to the lowest common denominator.

39
Talking straight
say what you mean, mean what you say

Many of us enjoy playing games. Some of these games, however, can impact seriously on our relationships. We may find we treat relationships as a game without rules. Perhaps the following conversation is familiar to you.

SALLY: Where were you last night? I called and you weren't there.
PAUL: I was out.
SALLY: I know that, but what did you do?
PAUL: Oh, I went out with some … er … friends.
SALLY: Who?
PAUL: You know, the usual gang …
SALLY: Did you go to the movies?
PAUL: No, just … er … out …

Do you get the impression that Paul is hiding something, that he's being evasive? He obviously doesn't want to give too much information away. For whatever reason he's not being honest. Here's another example:

TALKING STRAIGHT

BOSS: John, have you finished that report for this afternoon's meeting?
JOHN: Er, no, not yet, I'm still trying to collate some of the information.
BOSS: But you will have it finished by two o'clock, won't you?
JOHN: Oh, I'm sure of it, I'll try ...
BOSS: Try? Try isn't good enough. It just has to be finished.

It's clear that John is also covering up. He probably forgot all about the report, and is trying to make excuses. He's fudging, stalling for thinking time, and it's all quite transparent. Maybe he hopes the boss will let him off the hook. John isn't being honest and his responses only compound the problem. Maybe he'll get away with it; but what if he doesn't?

It's very easy to talk around a subject, to evade the point. Language can give the careful listener clues about our state of mind and the meaning behind the words. Take the first example above: it's easy to work out Paul's state of mind. Although he may be lying, he's probably also guilty by omission.

If we are not talking straight to friends, teachers, work associates,

> Another reason we do not talk straight is that we say what we think the other person wants to hear.

our spouses, we are being less than truthful and complicating our relationships. Often this sort of behaviour can be habit-forming. We get used to playing the game, skirting around the truth to see what we can get away with. Why do we do it? Sometimes we are avoiding confrontation. Take John and his boss. John could have gone to his boss and simply said that the work wasn't complete. Obviously

John was hoping that the problem would simply go away. But we can often solve problems by facing up to, and dealing with them, head-on.

Another reason we do not talk straight is that we say what we think the other person wants to hear. We say what we mean, but we don't really mean what we say. Here we are being manipulative. Again this is not talking straight, but playing a game. We may sometimes do this because telling only half the story enables us to retain power and some people find power and control important. However, power and control have little to do with maintaining straight or honest relationships.

Perhaps we avoid straight talk to protect someone else's feelings. Even though the truth may be hurtful, a little judgement will tell us when it's the appropriate time to talk straight. If someone we care for is in an unhealthy relationship, we can listen carefully and try to say something which indicates our understanding of their plight. Chances are the friend will appreciate it.

Often at work people really appreciate honesty. Many people in senior positions are surrounded by people who don't want to make waves by complaining or criticising. They may well think that someone who speaks out is refreshingly honest. If you have valid justification, go ahead and speak out, even if it means going against the consensus. You may well be respected for your courage. But don't speak too hastily, and don't speak just to boost your own ego. You must be able to justify your comments. On the other hand, if you are criticised for your honesty or for speaking out, you may not be in the right organisation. Why compromise your own integrity for political expedience? At some point you have to choose between the two.

Honesty seems to be in short supply these days, so make sure you say what you mean, *and* mean what you say.

40
Listening and understanding

Have you ever been in a situation where you thought you were having a conversation with someone but in fact all they were doing was talking at you? They're simply playing their own movie back to you, with you sitting there as a compliant audience, unable to participate in any two-way interaction. There is no genuine attempt to listen, let alone understand what you are trying to say or share your feelings about the matter being discussed.

It seems ironic that the person who is so often the one determined to give us advice and try to communicate is so poor at two of the key elements of relating and communicating—listening and understanding. It is often said that most people are poor listeners. They don't tune in to what the other person is saying. They get bored or are busy preparing their answer, or they think that the other person doesn't know what they are talking about. As a consequence of this superficial listening it is easy to miss an important opportunity to gain greater insight into how the other person feels and thinks about the subject being discussed. Yet it is through intent listening that we gain a deeper understanding of the other person, and in this understanding we can forge a closer relationship. To put it succinctly, people may hear the words you say, but may not actually listen or comprehend what you are saying.

Listening and Understanding

> ✯ Most of the time listening to others is a bit like trying to tune in to a radio station where we can't receive the signal very clearly.

In developing effective listening skills, the listener must have their own communication channels open and be careful not to allow their own assumptions or preconceptions to distort the messages being received. It is essential to be receptive to the message and also the way it is being communicated. We all communicate in different ways. Much depends on our mood, what we have to say, and the context in which we communicate.

It takes great care, skill and persistence to really listen carefully. It is especially difficult if we are not used to doing it. Most of the time listening to others is a bit like trying to tune in to a radio station where we can't receive the signal very clearly. There are lots of words (and interferences) coming through, some sounding jumbled, and we really have to tune in very carefully to understand what has been said and meant. We have to be alert to the range of signals people send out and train ourselves to become aware of their meaning.

Many times, of course, it's easier just to listen to ourselves talk. It could also be that we don't want to listen to others because we have decided that they have nothing worthwhile or important to say. This belief can act as an immediate block to our understanding. The truth is that regardless of who the person is, their background, social standing, occupation (or lack of one), friends, financial status, every person has their 'own story' and a right to be heard. One of the most difficult skills is burying our own prejudices and opening our minds to the possibility that others have something valid or worthwhile to say. This generally requires us to make a significant shift in our thinking and not simply try to be 'right' all the time.

We need to examine our reasons for always jumping in, for cutting people short, for not being prepared to listen and understand. In order to make a genuine effort to listen, to think about and integrate what other people are saying to us, we need to be able to listen to and understand what our own inner voices are saying. We can then more effectively listen to others.

Once we start to really listen to others, we might be surprised by what we pick up. All sorts of messages may come across, telling us more than we ever knew about the other person and how they feel and wish to relate. We have begun to respond to their non-verbal communication, and to recognise that what they don't say may be as important (or perhaps more important) than what they do say. Now we can really begin to understand people, not as objects or things to be conquered or controlled, but as separate persons with their own attitudes, beliefs, feelings, and complexities which are as valid and as real as our own.

Even though it is hard work, learning to listen to other people will help us build stronger and more lasting relationships, which may become a real source of joy and contentment, bringing us as much insight into ourselves as we have into others. It's a skill worth acquiring and a journey well worth taking, because you'll always learn more by listening than by talking.

41
Negotiation and conflict resolution

In chapter 39, we discussed 'talking straight'. Another component of talking straight is negotiation and conflict resolution. Negotiation can be as simple as buying a car, or as complex as negotiating a pay rise, or even conducting political and international negotiations.

Throughout our lives, whether we realise it or not, we are constantly involved in negotiations, often formally but more often informally, in the form of discussions with family and friends. We sometimes even have to negotiate with ourselves, trying to resolve inner conflicts. The same rules apply.

There does seem to be some reluctance in our society to negotiate for a 'better deal' on a regular basis. We tend to think of negotiating as something to be saved for markets and car-buying, but why not apply it to other goods or services? 'Can you give me a better price than that?' It doesn't hurt to ask. So what if they knock off 10%: it may not seem like much, but it's a few dollars in your pocket. If, over twelve months, you negotiate regularly, the savings can add up to a tidy sum.

Some of us are better at negotiating than others. Regardless of how good or bad we think we are, how many of us really understand what negotiating is and what we want to achieve from it? So often it seems that we are more interested in protecting our entrenched position and want to negotiate to win at all costs; it's part of our competitive streak. This simply leads to a breakdown in negotiations, often with a lot of resulting conflict.

Conflict resulting from a breakdown in communications can lead to all sorts of difficulties, because many people find conflict of any kind very difficult to deal with. For whatever reason, we want to run away from it. Even though we believe that such behaviour is conflict resolution, it is really nothing more than conflict avoidance. Such behaviour keeps us a prisoner, locked into dealing (or not dealing) with problems and situations in the same old ways. It certainly doesn't improve our negotiation skills at all.

> In thinking about negotiations it is always important to try to depersonalise the issues and find some common ground.

In thinking about negotiations it is always important to try to depersonalise the issues (while recognising the make-up of the personalities involved) and find some common ground. This can be a useful starting point for any negotiation. In other words, let's discover what we already agree on and what's left to negotiate. It is also important to understand the consequences of not reaching a negotiated position or resolving our conflicts. Where will this leave us and how will we feel?

The way we negotiate and try to resolve conflicts tells us as much about the type of person we are as it does about our perceptions of and attitudes towards the person we are negotiating with. If, for example, we think someone is a weak negotiator and we can easily get what we want by

NEGOTIATION AND CONFLICT RESOLUTION

> ✯
> One of the most difficult issues in negotiating is to avoid treating it as some sort of competition with winners and losers.

intimidating them, the way we negotiate with them is likely to reflect our attitude. By contrast, if we come up against a person who appears to be very tough and aggressive, we might feel somewhat intimidated to the point where we tend to give in very easily. In the first situation, we may be guilty of abusing our position simply to achieve our own ends. In the second, we may be left feeling empty and somewhat abused ourselves.

One of the most difficult issues in negotiating is to avoid treating it as some sort of competition with winners and losers. We need to take into account the other person's needs rather than simply feeling we've beaten them. We must learn to view the negotiation as a partnership, where we want to see that the other person is as satisfied with the end result as we are.

It's vital to be able to apply to negotiations some of the skills learnt in other chapters of this book; listening and understanding in particular. Similarly, trying to tune into what the other person is *not* saying, as well as listening to what they *are* saying, can provide us with valuable information in our negotiations and conflict resolution.

We need to understand our own position and what we want to achieve in a particular negotiation. What is our preferred outcome, and what degree of conflict are we prepared to engage in to achieve our desired outcome?

When we find ourselves in difficult negotiations or conflicts, it is essential that we find our own way of introducing some space (and time) into the situation, so that we are not swallowed up or simply ambushed. It is

NEGOTIATION AND CONFLICT RESOLUTION

critical that throughout the whole process we are able to retain a sense of purpose and integrity, and that our ability to achieve the outcome we desire permits us to work through the difficulties. If there is no compromise or resolution in sight, we can either accept the situation or, if need be, walk away from it. Keep a perspective on the situation, without getting emotionally tangled up. Stay objective where possible, and keep a clear head. This will help you to work through and understand what the emotional issues are and what part they are playing in the negotiation.

It's also important to note that conflict does have a positive side. It alerts us to problems, brings them out into the open and allows us to work towards a solution. This applies to conflict from within or from without. Conflict can act as a stimulus to improve a situation, such as your job or your relationship. As we said before, it turns a problem into an opportunity.

Here are some fundamental points to remember when you're negotiating:

- Try to ensure that both parties win. It's not a winner-takes-all event.
- It's a matter of give and take. You may need to concede a few points.
- If you agree to concede, ask the other party to concede something as well. 'If I agree to do that, what will you agree to?'
- You don't have to accept the first offer.
- If you are buying something like a car (where negotiation is part of the game), don't be too obvious in your desire for the car. Be cool and relaxed.
- Be prepared to walk away from the deal.

42
Beware the hidden agenda

This chapter is about ulterior or possibly 'interior' motives, the hidden agendas in our lives. In many cases, individuals have hidden agendas, families have them, organisations and governments have them. For example, a shopping mall developer may decide to build a brand new mall in an outer suburb. The press release states that the developer is interested in 'revitalising the local community'. The hidden agenda here is that the developer sees a dollar in it; he can make a profit, and along the way the community may indeed be revitalised. But to come out publicly and admit the profit motive would be unwise. The development needs to be 'sold' on a more altruistic, community-based level.

Or, in another example, I might attend a basketball game simply to meet someone who I know is a basketball fan. My hidden agenda is the meeting rather than the game. So, we often have ulterior motives for our actions. Even if we don't recognise them at the time, we should be aware of them in ourselves and in others. The skill is

> ✯
> Often, coming across a hidden agenda is like falling into a deep pit, especially if you didn't fall, but were pushed.

BEWARE THE HIDDEN AGENDA

to recognise the hidden agenda for what it is and deal with that directly, rather than dealing with some more or less acceptable veneer of truth. By identifying the hidden agenda we can go direct to the heart of the situation without being distracted or having the 'wool pulled over our eyes'.

Ken was recently bypassed for a promotion. He was desperate for the promotion, but somebody else was appointed. Ken learnt that the person who won the position had some relevant extra qualifications that Ken didn't have. The appointment was a simple choice based on straightforward criteria. Ken initially accepted that, but over the next few weeks he felt there was more to it. He couldn't sleep at night; he became nervous and irritated. He decided to have a long talk with his boss. He discovered that he didn't get the promotion for a number of unexpected reasons. The hidden agenda was at work.

First of all, Ron, who won the promotion, won it because he was related to one of the senior managers. Ken's boss was trying to get an overseas posting and the easiest way of getting this posting was to employ Ron. Ken's boss apologised saying simply 'Well, that's business ... ' Ken resigned. He felt he had been a pawn in his boss's chess-game. The hidden agenda was clear. Ken was an expendable resource, one that his boss could dispense with to further his own career. He was in a no-win situation. He is now self-employed and much happier. He has nobody else's hidden agenda to worry about.

Often, coming across a hidden agenda is like falling into a deep pit, especially if you didn't fall, but were pushed.

So, how do you work out if there is a hidden agenda? It's important to note that they're not called hidden agendas for nothing. They are hidden, often deeply and invisibly like a computer virus, slowly corrupting and changing the nature of a particular situation.

Beware the Hidden Agenda

More often than not, like Ken, you'll discover the hidden agenda when it's too late; it has already firmly taken hold. All you are left with are the consequences. One way of detecting a hidden agenda is to use your imagination and intuition. Does X have any other motive for doing this? Has Y done this for reasons other than those stated? You may even have friends or associates you can talk to. Try to keep things in perspective even so. Don't simply believe that everybody is out to get you, and that every meeting that takes place concerns your future, or that you are a victim, a pawn in somebody else's game. But if you *are* a victim of somebody else's manipulation, it's better that you find out sooner rather than later.

Hidden agendas in intimate relationships just don't work. The terms are almost mutually exclusive. How can you hope to have an honest, loving relationship when some ulterior motive constantly lurks in the background? Hidden agendas have no part to play here. The foundation of integrity which is the very basis of such relationships will crack and crumble under the strain of double standards.

In this part of the book we have written about honesty, and a code of behaviour that forms a basis for living with a sense of purpose and integrity. Honesty is the antithesis of the hidden agenda. A hidden agenda cannot operate in a totally honest environment. It needs to feed off deceit, intrigue and mystery. Beware the hidden agenda both within yourself and within others as you begin to discover what motivates yourself and others.

43
Body language
the hidden clues

We are all aware of body language. A frown, the angle of a head, the expression on a face, the position of the hands. It's all non-verbal communication. We can see if a person is tense or relaxed, confident or despondent. A good place to observe body language is cartoons. You'll see the funniest and most exaggerated examples of body language as the characters try to get out of ridiculous situations. In movies, too, you'll see stereotypical characters behave over and over again with the same sort of body language. Dracula would move differently to someone playing a happy-go-lucky character. A murderous villain would, especially in silent movies, be seen to rub his hands together very slowly as an evil grin erupts on his face. But the same character rubbing his hands together quickly would give the scene a whole new meaning. Maybe he's simply cold. Watch an old Western. The bad guy doesn't often smile, and he swaggers a certain way. His body language, and the clothes he wears, are telling you to keep out of his way.

> Dracula would move differently to someone playing a happy-go-lucky character.

BODY LANGUAGE

Body language is important because it reflects the state of mind of a person long before they confirm it verbally. Perhaps someone at a meeting is sitting there looking at you with their arms tightly folded. The chances are that they are taking a negative approach. They are closed to information and are unlikely to budge. On the other hand, this person could also be concentrating on what you are saying and folded arms might just be a habit. So while we shouldn't fall into the trap of making body language too predictable, or jumping to conclusions, having a grasp of body language can be very helpful in all sorts of situations from job interviews to asking someone out on a date, or having a conversation with a friend or acquaintance.

> Watch the way people at parties give us clues.

Let's take the job interview as an example. Here are some characteristics of two different interviewers. You'll very quickly be able to judge which person is more likely to make the applicant a job offer.

Interviewer one: Arms folded, leaning back in the chair. Blank facial expression. Sometimes folds arms behind head. Does not take notes. Does not appear to be listening or making eye contact. Acts very fidgety, glances regularly at watch. Often cuts answers short. Is in a hurry to end interview.

Interviewer two: Leans forward. Takes notes. Asks questions, smiles. Concentrates on what the interviewee is saying. Allows the talk to flow freely. Is fully engaged in a two-way conversation.

Who would you rather talk with?

Watch the way people at parties give us clues as to how interested they are in the conversation. If we are boring somebody, they tend to look around rather than look at us.

They may fidget and look at their watch, a sign that it's time to move on to somebody who may be more interested in what you have to say, or vice versa.

When you are talking to someone, it's important to maintain eye contact, though without looking like a zombie or as if you are staring blankly. By establishing eye contact you lock onto and into the other person. You are listening and talking to each other and nobody else. Perhaps eye contact is also a very subtle form of non-verbal communication where each party is attempting to assess the other person's sincerity.

We've probably all met people who don't 'look you in the eye'. Eye contact is a crucial communications tool. If you are, for example, asking a friend for urgent help, eye contact can help establish your sincerity and urgency. When you first meet someone, you may momentarily look away. You are avoiding that 'locking on', because locking on might indicate more interest than you want to show.

It's also very difficult to fake your body language, because faking is in itself body language that tells the other person that you are faking. The true body language always tends to come through. Think about people you don't really trust, or consider to be a little 'shifty' (in fact 'shifty' often refers to lack of eye contact). Compare their behaviour and body language to those you rely on and trust. We admire good acting so much because both the verbal and non-verbal communication is so convincing. The heroine does look grief-stricken when her lover leaves town. The hero does look like he's going to take revenge on the bad guy. Just look at his expression; we know what he's thinking, all right.

> Watch politicians to see if they mean what they say.

BODY LANGUAGE

By concentrating on the other person and being aware of their body language, we can go a long way to establishing clearer verbal communications. During election time, watch politicians to see if they mean what they say. Their nervous body language can be a giveaway and can win or lose votes. For people in public positions, body language can be even more important than verbal communication, and we can often tune into it faster. So stay alert for clues when you talk to people; you can gain some valuable insights.

44
Inner space, outer space

From time to time we need to create a sense of space in our inner world. We need to assess, examine and understand ourselves in order to apply that understanding to our relationships and to the interactions in our daily lives. Indeed, the way we understand and treat ourselves will have a major impact on how we relate to and treat others. It will affect the quality of our relationships. Creating a sense of inner space is akin to providing ourselves with an oasis, a physical and mental place to which we can go when we feel crowded or unsure of our emotional response to others or to the outside world generally.

> Creating a sense of inner space is akin to providing ourselves with an oasis.

We may often feel crowded out or intimidated by the behaviour of others. If we find it difficult to have a sense of space between ourselves and the other person, we can end up being caught in another's 'web', seemingly being their 'object', and not knowing why. Maybe we are eager to please or wish to seem agreeable to another person or we may simply feel anxious about ourselves. Whatever the reason, when we are confronted by someone whom we find intimidating, we need to introduce some space, particularly mental space, between that person and ourselves. Otherwise, we may feel trapped in some way and go along for the ride, only to feel injured, used or abused in some way after the encounter. We are also likely to feel equally bad about ourselves, for letting ourselves down or for being dragged into the mess.

Paula had always seen herself as an approval-seeking person. She would always try to avoid conflicts and confrontations. When she got into these situations, she would go into 'approval overdrive' and believe they were all her fault. Without even thinking about the issues, or how she felt about the matter, she would take the blame and apologise in order to calm the waters. Over the years, such behaviour had led many people to take advantage of her. Rather than taking time to examine what was going on inside her and how she felt, she would dismiss her feelings as unimportant and move into approval mode, confusing her needs with those of others, becoming the object in the relationship and losing her sense of subjectivity.

Even when she thought that someone's behaviour may have been manipulative, she allowed herself to be caught in what were often very complicated and messy relationships and situations. She left herself no space, inner or outer, in which to reflect on, or understand, what was happening. Generally, after such encounters Paula would feel nothing except horribly used and somewhat abused and angry. Time and time again she would blame herself for being caught in such situations.

Paula had been working in an organisation for some time but had recently changed departments. Her new boss, Rachel, had recently joined the company and seemed interested in Paula as a person, not simply as a worker. Whilst working on a particular project, Rachel asked Paula what she thought about an idea for the project—how did she feel about it? Paula didn't know what to say. She wasn't used to being asked for her opinion. The request was confronting and difficult for Paula to accept. Now Paula was required to trust her own judgement and feel that her opinion was as valuable as anybody else's. After some thought, Paula responded to Rachel's request and provided some very insightful and interesting ideas which Rachel later adopted.

Over the next few months, Paula gained confidence in offering her views, based not so much on what other people expected her to say, or would approve, but based on what she herself thought and felt about a particular issue. Paula has learnt that in creating a sense of inner space for herself, she has created the basis for developing greater insight and self-knowledge, rather than merely reacting to people. She is now able to apply this skill not only in reaching a better understanding of herself but also in improving the quality of her relationships, without sacrificing her own sense of integrity or purpose.

Paula's experience shows us that the more insight you can develop by creating an inner space, the easier it may be to recognise and understand your own desires and motivations. Once you can create this space you will not be totally crowded out by your own or others' feelings, responses, thoughts and actions. This is a skill you can apply to the world around you. Instead of being overwhelmed by situations and people, and responding in a way which does nothing to help your sense of self, you can learn to create an outer space. In this space you can reflect on how you want to react to others. One way of developing this ability is through meditation, through finding a place where you can be quietly alone. A worthwhile skill is to 'empty' yourself of thoughts and emotions and calm the inner chatter. This will help you focus on real issues in your life, filtering out fears and imaginings. Practised regularly, meditation can create a sense of inner space and can allow you to respond to the outside world in a way which genuinely reflects your inner feelings.

Knowing how to create a sense of inner and outer space can have a significant impact on how we feel about ourselves and on the quality of our relationships with others. Why? Because the way we respond to people reflects an understanding of who we are, and as a consequence the quality, honesty and integrity of our communication will be better. Relationships and awkward situations may not feel any easier but at least they will be more honest. We will have a basis for developing as individuals while still being connected to those we are close to and love. Creating both the inner and outer space to achieve this can be a remarkable and rewarding experience.

Part 5

Living and working

45
Recognising strengths
accepting and dealing with weaknesses

Every person on this planet has strengths and weaknesses. It's part of being human. The problem is that quite often we don't recognise, understand or appreciate these qualities in ourselves or others. If from a young age we are told about our weaknesses, we may have developed an acute sense of what they are. But we probably do not have a very strong sense of our strengths. They may be difficult to recognise or acknowledge.

If we recognised our strengths, if we could embrace them, they could propel us forward and work for us. Similarly, if we recognised our weaknesses, and understood why they were weaknesses, we might learn to accept and deal with them. We could stop them being like millstones around our necks, constantly holding us back from achieving our potential. Do

> ✯
> Do we really feel that we know our strengths and weaknesses? Or are we merely relying on someone else's assessment of them?

Recognising strengths and weaknesses

we really feel that we know our strengths and weaknesses? Or are we merely relying on someone else's assessment of them? To rely on others to help us understand ourselves may be dangerous. Abdicating our responsibility for understanding our strengths and weaknesses, and relying on somebody else's interpretation, may have all sorts of unintended consequences. This may be more likely if we don't have a strong sense of our own self. Because we are all different, what one person might consider a strength another may consider a weakness.

It is essential that we begin by recognising and understanding our own strengths and weaknesses. We should be clear about what we are good at and similarly, be clear and accepting of what we are not so good at. That way we can concentrate on building strength in those areas that need attention and ensuring that our weaknesses don't hold us back. We can do this by understanding our underlying behaviour.

Richard always appeared to be a positive sort of person. He never seemed to worry. He never spoke to anyone about his weaknesses or fears. But since his school days Richard had developed a habit that he had never been able to overcome. He could never finish anything he started. Whether it was an assignment for school, an essay, a course at university or a major project at work—nothing would ever be finished. Richard didn't recognise any problem or weakness; he just got bored with a task and then couldn't be bothered finishing it. Even if the consequences of not finishing it were pretty bad, this didn't seem to fuss him.

In other areas of his life, for example in helping his friends or trying to be a good listener, Richard seemed able to recognise his strengths even though he didn't think about them much. But when it came to recognising weaknesses, those things he needed to

RECOGNISING STRENGTHS AND WEAKNESSES

change, he seemed to have a closed mind. It was clear to others that Richard's problem was holding him back in major areas of his life. To this day, Richard continues to miss promotions and to change jobs pretty regularly. Even at home, where he has started certain renovations, nothing is ever completed. It has got to the point where it is frustrating and affecting Richard more than others around him but he says he can't change things: that's just the way he is.

Indeed, Richard is probably unlikely to change things until he can look within himself and accept that his inability to finish things is a weakness that is holding him back and having an unfortunate impact in lots of areas of his life. He needs to see that the weakness is not something that he needs to be 'ashamed' of but something that can be dealt with by trying to understand what it represents and what other facets of his life may be connected to it. Once Richard is prepared to make the initial shift by beginning to recognise and accept the pattern of behaviour as a weakness, he will be able to deal with it more effectively and eventually to change. He needs to do this in a way that looks at the weaknesses not in any judgemental or 'bad' way, but simply as it is, for what it is.

Dealing with weaknesses, no matter how entrenched they are, can, over time, be extremely enlightening and liberating. It can facilitate great progress and allow you to focus much more on strengths. Of course to make such a shift takes skill and patience as well as an ability to be honest and open with oneself in a way that one may not previously have been able or prepared to be. It's little wonder that it seems easier just to stay in our safe and friendly groove, and fail to recognise that things can be different.

Dealing with strengths can be less confronting because of the positive impact they have in our lives. But it is important to ensure that we don't focus on our strengths in a way that becomes an excuse for not dealing with our weaknesses. That way we will end up undermining or limiting our strengths as well.

46
Planned vs unplanned careers
keeping your options open

Is it really possible to plan your career and still keep your options open? Like so many aspects of life, a career is often a question of balance. As we have said before, we can plan everything down to the last detail or we can plan the overall shape and direction of our lives, leaving sufficient room for flexibility, spontaneity and the unexpected. Let's have a look at how Prue and Jason, two very different people, tried to manage their lives, especially their careers.

Prue always wanted to be a marketing executive. In planning her career she left nothing to chance. Every step of her career had been mapped out in her attempt to plan every move and timetable every promotion. In such a well-planned life there was no room for error, no room for flexibility, mistakes or things that weren't in the plan. But more than this, there was no room or possibility in her plan for others to change their minds or make life difficult for Prue. There were no other options if things went wrong.

PLANNED VS UNPLANNED CAREERS

Jason, on the other hand, was the opposite. Nothing in his life was ever planned or thought through too deeply. Everything was a bit of a serendipitous adventure. He would take things as they came and simply see what happened. If things worked out then that was fine; if they didn't, well it didn't really matter as he could always move on to the next thing, whatever that was. He viewed his career in the same manner. Wherever the next fix came from that would be fine. For Jason life was a game. The fact was that Jason was only fooling himself. Nobody else really cared about his career; nobody else lost any sleep over whether he looked after himself, or succeeded or not. The problem was that Jason didn't seem to care much either. So paradoxically, while he thought he had lots of options he didn't really have any; his choices were rapidly shrinking. Unless he began to look at the direction of his life and to think carefully about what was important, the viable options would become extremely limited very quickly.

Even though Prue and Jason are in many ways opposites, some of the issues confronting them are similar. The fact that one has such a totally planned life and the other has a totally unstructured existence tells us a great deal about them as people. Sure, their individual traits are highlighted very starkly in their careers but, whether they like it or not, both are finding their options are limited. For Prue, there is no deviating from her plan. There are no other options, there can never be any prospect of anything not working out or being any different from what is planned. This is the way it is and will be—that's it! For Prue, with her life totally planned and structured, who needs other options?

Jason's view can be summarised as 'Who cares about having any options?' He probably considers that he has all the options he needs (though he doesn't need any; life just unfolds as it will). He doesn't need to interfere, shape or guide his life because whatever happens will happen. For

Planned vs Unplanned Careers

Jason, what more options could he possibly want? After all, he's a free spirit.

For Jason and Prue, the important issue is one of balance. Neither being fixated on the plan or letting things simply happen will help them achieve their goals. They need to work out what they want to do, what is important, and then put in place the appropriate framework. At some point, Jason must recognise that his approach will simply ensure that his life goes round and round in circles. He has to sort out his priorities and take the steps consistent with them. Until he begins the arduous task of deciding what direction his life (and career) should take, a plan is

> Your plan needs to be a guide. You shouldn't become such a slave to it that you end up totally preoccupied with the planning and leave no time for doing and enjoying.

unlikely to be of much use. In Prue's case, while it is okay for her to have a plan which charts the direction she wants her life to take, she needs flexibility and room to manoeuvre.

Your plan needs to be a guide. You shouldn't become such a slave to it that you end up totally preoccupied with the planning and leave no time for doing and enjoying. Perhaps Prue needs to experience a few things not going according to her plan to understand the real value of planning and having more than one option.

You may well ask why is it so important to keep your options open? Why do you need them? Aren't they just likely to confuse the situation? Isn't it better to try to plan as much as possible? Too many options may, at times, confuse us but they also can provide the basis for real choice. As we have said before, if you understand what motivates you and what is important to you, then your planning is likely to include more choices. This doesn't mean that you have to act on all or any of the available options. But if things don't work out according to plan, then you may have some insight into why. There will be other options if you so desire.

Imagine a town that was over-planned. There would be no options because everything would be planned leaving no possibility to respond to changing circumstances. Imagine a totally unplanned town. Here there would be no options either, because ultimately everything would be such a mess everything would need to be pulled down and started again.

Of course, planning or not planning pervades every aspect of our life, not simply our careers. Sometimes we try to over-plan the course of our relationships or even our leisure time. Such over-planning can end up strangling relationships and other activities to the point where they lack any spontaneity or enjoyment. Life becomes heavy, predictable and unlikely to be a source of much real joy. As with so many skills we acquire in life, the question of planning careers is intimately connected to all other areas of life, including the way we think, our emotional needs and responses and the need to retain a sense of balance and space.

In chapter 20 we discussed preparing your mission statement. By developing some overall plan, you can shape the direction of your life in as much detail as you see fit. Some plan is better than no plan, and a map, even a very simple one, can help reinforce and give direction, purpose and meaning to your mission statement.

47
Opportunity knocks

It's true, opportunity does knock. Sometimes it comes crashing right into your life, or it lurks around the corner waiting for you to discover it. At other times opportunity seems to desert us altogether. Opportunity can sometimes be called 'luck', or 'good fortune' or simply 'being in the right place at the right time'.

Some opportunities are very clear and obvious, such as a promotion, or an offer to work overseas. Then the problem is not to create or find opportunities; it's weighing up the quality of the opportunity. An offer may seem like an opportunity, but you may have to pay too high a price. When you look a little deeper, you may even realise that the offer is not really an opportunity at all. It may be tempting to jump right in and say 'yes', but try to take the time to weigh up the pros and cons. Look at the opportunity in detail and see how it fits into your overall plan.

Opportunity can manifest itself in very strange ways indeed. Sometimes it arrives wrapped in a cloak of 'bad news'. It's only later, often much later, that we say that the event 'was actually the best thing that ever happened.'

Take Gina, for example. She wanted to enrol in a teaching course. She always liked art and set her sights on becoming an art teacher. Due to the quota system, and the fact that her results weren't quite up to scratch, Gina missed out on a place. She was devastated. All her hopes were dashed. She wasn't going to become an art teacher. Within a few months however Gina found an interesting job at an art gallery. Within two years she was the manager of the gallery curating exhibitions for other artists. She certainly now feels that not becoming an art teacher was the best thing that ever happened. At the time it was very difficult for Gina to interpret missing out on a teaching place as an opportunity to discover something new or take a new direction, but that's exactly what happened.

More often than not, opportunities, both large and small, aren't necessarily going to tap you on the shoulder. Just as you have to be your own engine of change, you must be prepared to create opportunities for yourself, or be vigilant for spotting opportunities that you can take advantage of. Your state of mind needs to be pro-active, seeking out opportunities wherever possible. If you are content simply to react and wait for opportunities to surface, you may spend your whole life waiting for that 'golden opportunity'.

So, there are two basic attitudes towards opportunity. One is to recognise it, and run with it; the other is to create your own opportunities. Forget about the 'Cinderella factor'. There are no fairy godmothers who are going to leap in and save the day while you're moping about how 'unlucky' you are. The Cinderella approach will achieve nothing except keeping you stuck. You need to accept responsibility for your own future, regardless of how difficult that may be. Don't wait for the government, or anybody else, to step in and wave the magic wand. It won't happen. You need to initiate change yourself.

Being alert to opportunities takes some practice and insight. It's a bit like getting used to the dark, where you start seeing things that other people can't. A chance meeting at a party, a phone call from a long-lost friend who now works in

OPPORTUNITY KNOCKS

a similar industry, an encounter at a coffee-shop, these seemingly trivial incidents can lead to opportunity creation. But you have to be prepared to be enthusiastic, do the hard work and follow through. Have a target in mind. By that we mean be clear about what you want to achieve. You need to ask yourself if there is an opportunity lurking just below the surface. Once you spot it, no matter how slim a sliver of an opportunity, just go for it.

> Once you spot it, no matter how slim a sliver of an opportunity, just go for it.

Jerry runs his own advertising consultancy. One night he and some friends were out at a local motor show, looking at the display of new cars. Rick was there with his fibreglass kit-car display. Jerry's friends all asked details about the car, brakes, price and so on. Jerry asked just one question: 'Who does your advertising?' That one question eventually led to Jerry picking up a new account. He saw an opportunity and he took it. Sometimes you have to be prepared to put the fear of rejection to one side, and just go for it.

Creating opportunities for yourself is also about learning to take control of your life and understanding how you respond in such situations. For some people, the desire to call the shots, make the decisions and shape the outcome can be an important motivation. Perhaps you want to set up your own business. Taking evening or part-time courses could improve your knowledge and create career opportunities.

By creating your own opportunities, you are also creating your own tomorrow. Be alert to opportunities and be prepared to seize them. Just one could change your life.

48
A job
career path or dead end?

You might ask, what's the difference between a job and a career? How important is a 'career path'? The difference between a job and career is quite significant. A job is generally something you do to make a dollar. Summer vacation work is often just a job. You work at a garage, a supermarket, a fast food chain. It's a job that will earn you some money, but rarely is it a career. A job very rarely has a clear career path stretching out before you. Ahead is generally more of the same. A career has the potential to provide for personal growth. (Later in this chapter we'll also take a look at actually getting paid to enjoy yourself.)

> ✯ Where will you be in one year, or five years' time? Do you feel trapped? Can you change things?

It's also true that some people can have a career, but still view it as just a 'job' and be bored with it. There is no hard and fast rule, or guarantee that one area of work will give you more satisfaction than another. The answer will always come back to what you want, what you need and how you choose to express yourself. It's what is important to you that counts, not a label that says 'career' or 'job'.

A JOB

Whether or not you have a career or a job isn't as critical as whether or not you are staring at a dead end. Once again, we ask you to use your imagination and put yourself into 'fast-forward'. Where will you be in one year, or five years' time? Will your work give you the kind of nourishment that you are looking for? Will it suit your personality? Do you feel trapped? Can you change things? The sort of person you are will dictate your direction. Jobs and careers can equally be rewarding or a dead end ... a conveyor belt to nowhere.

Karen thought she was lucky to get a job. She was nineteen and very keen. The job was with her state environment protection authority. Karen worked in an office that checked vehicle emissions and worked on policy matters. After about a year she felt trapped. She liked working in an environmental area, but felt that she wasn't doing enough, just shuffling pieces of paper from one side of a desk to another. She went to the human resources manager. They spoke for a while about the sort of things Karen liked doing. She almost shyly admitted she liked working with plants and being outdoors. The manager asked Karen if she had ever considered going to a horticultural college to learn about plants and gardening. Karen thought this was a great idea, made some inquiries and discovered there was a twelve-month evening course, followed by a year of full-time study. Karen stayed at the environment protection authority during the course (the money came in very handy) and the following year commenced full-time study. She shifted back home with her parents for that year, and today Karen is working as a landscape gardener. She is outdoors and working with plants, often seven days a week. She is no longer bored: she has found work that suits her and allows her to express herself.

Not all of us are as lucky as Karen in finding something that suits us. Some trial and error is almost inevitable. If you are a student, and unsure about your work options, experiment a little. Where possible, over summer vacations try different jobs, even if it means starting at the bottom. Get your hands dirty by sampling a few jobs and careers. Speak to people about their experiences and develop some insight into why people like or dislike their jobs. Knowing your strengths and weaknesses can help eliminate some false starts. It can create some priorities for you too. If you dislike the idea of working with your hands, learning a trade may not be sensible. If you don't like working with numbers, accounting could be a problem. If you like animals, becoming a vet is a possibility and so on.

Choosing to change a career or job may mean that you have to go down a few rungs on the ladder. You may earn less than some of your friends, but if you are doing what you really want to be doing, this hardly matters. Indeed, if you enjoy what you are doing, and are earning a reasonable living, you are way ahead of the majority of the population, who simply have a paying job that doesn't particularly interest or stimulate them. Perhaps you can now appreciate that while the difference between a job or career can be blurred, it's your own satisfaction that's important.

Even if it's not easy to find exactly the sort of work you want, keep trying, and keep some balance by getting some quality into your life in other areas. Be flexible and be prepared to change. Don't stick with a job just because you feel it's secure and it's too hard or risky to look for something else. This is your life and livelihood that we are talking about. Don't get stuck in that rut, but then again don't make a habit of shifting around either, just for the sake of a change. It's quite common for people to swap courses and faculties at university. People change careers. Doctors become best-selling authors, teachers become musicians, soldiers become public speakers. Just avoid that dead end,

A JOB

and don't be immobilised by fear of change. You can always minimise the risk by lining up something else before 'jumping ship', but keep moving forward, not for the sake of an extra dollar, but for your own development and self-esteem.

> ✹ Working smart is more important than working hard.

When you find the right sort of work or career-path, you'll actually feel that you are getting paid to enjoy yourself. But you need to work 'smart'. Working smart is more important than working hard. Are you still following an outmoded work ethic? Do you keep your head down, work hard and hope you'll be rewarded? Many people work hard, day in and day out, making enormous sacrifices in the belief that they will be handsomely rewarded. The truth is that many people are not being rewarded appropriately for their hard work. Combine working smart with working hard and you have a truly potent mixture.

Many people are fortunate enough to work smart. Of course the work can be hard and stressful at times, but there can be a lot of rewards as well. Take the Hollywood film director who pours a year or two of her life into a project. She's working hard, but she's also getting a lot of satisfaction at the same time. Take the best-selling fiction author who may take a year of quiet patience to churn out a book. He'll work eight hours a day, five days a week, just writing a book. The book will sell four million copies worldwide, earning him a handsome royalty, not to mention that the film rights to his novel may earn him another handsome amount. Not bad for one year's work. These are extreme and unusual examples, but they illustrate the difference between just working hard and working smart.

The people in the previous two examples are also getting

A JOB

paid to enjoy themselves. They have followed their passion. Imagine working in an area of work that you love, where a hobby or an obsession has become a source, not only of income, but of endless fascination and vitality. Film directors become directors because they love working with film, and people, and they love to tell stories with film. Many surgeons, for example, love what they do because of the satisfaction they gain from saving or extending a person's life. Many teachers love to teach and to watch their students learn and develop. For these people, and thousands more like them, 'Monday-itis' just doesn't exist. Some of them don't even care how much they get paid. They almost feel guilty to charge for their services. Something inside them pushes them along this path, regardless of what others may say or think.

Take a look at your own life. Is there anything there: an interest, a hobby, a secret passion, that you would like to turn into a viable living? Has anybody ever told you to 'Get a real job', or 'Why not do something constructive with your life'? Do you have a general impression that jobs and work should be dreary and mundane and think you should feel guilty if you actually enjoy what you do every day?

The way we work is changing very rapidly. Technology now allows us to work from home as efficiently (probably more so) as at an office. Where we work is becoming increasingly irrelevant. You can fax information to the office, or send it by modem. The same technology is opening up vastly new ways of working, ways that, as little as ten years ago, we never dreamed possible. We are required to work less with our hands in menial repetitive jobs, and more with our brains. Once we find the sort of work that helps define who we are, that motivates and challenges us, and gives meaning to our lives, the emotional, financial and intellectual rewards will seem to flow almost effortlessly.

A JOB

Put simply, if you can earn a living doing what you truly enjoy then you can still count yourself as being in the lucky minority. The strange thing is that once you find something you enjoy doing, you will end up working harder than ever. You know what it's like when you're doing something enjoyable: suddenly three hours have gone by and you haven't even realised it.

You'll also find that artificial barriers, such as the traditional nine-to-five working day and Monday-to-Friday will vanish, or become blurred and irrelevant. You'll work when you want to. You'll always manage to strike a balance between work and play, especially if you are self-employed. You can take the afternoon off, because you know that you have the option of working in the evening. You will tend to see your day in twelve-hour lumps, seven days a week, but with a more flexible structure. Some time is spent playing, relaxing and having a good time, and some time is spent working. How you carve up your time becomes less important because work and play become less distinct and flow into each other ... That's the future.

Look long and hard for something you really like to do, find a career that you can plug into, and get paid to enjoy yourself.

49
Climbing the ladder
just watch the grease

This chapter should perhaps be called 'The games we play', because, in many organisations, climbing the ladder often has more to do with gamesmanship than with talent and plain hard work. Competitiveness and hidden agendas are often involved, as we have seen in previous chapters. And we can quote again from the *Tao Te Ching*, 'Whether you move up or down the ladder, your position is still shaky.' It's only when our two feet are firmly on the ground that we can find true stability.

> Careers often resemble a game of Snakes 'n' Ladders. Climb the ladders, but slide down the snakes.

Climbing the ladder in your chosen vocation or career is seldom easy. Careers often resemble a game of Snakes 'n' Ladders. Climb the ladders, but slide down the snakes. But 'career ladders' come in all sorts of shapes and sizes. Some can be simply horizontal; some have rungs which suddenly break. You move along a ladder, but you don't seem to get very far. Other ladders are circular and you appear to keep going around and around. Some ladders are very short, just a few rungs and they stop; while some ladders aren't ladders at all—they're more like smooth, polished slides. The kind of career ladder that you have is often up to you and the type of job you have. Many jobs are 'dead end' as they have limited growth potential.

Let's assume that you want to get ahead in your chosen field of work. How do you ensure that you keep moving in the right direction and at a suitable pace? For a start, it certainly helps if you like what you are doing and are naturally motivated by the work. It also helps if the organisation you are with encourages personal growth and promotion, where promotion is based on performance rather than seniority.

A number of factors can hold you back, and these factors reflect the reality of working in a competitive world. Office politics, back-stabbing and strange hidden agendas can often block your career. There may be people in the organisation who simply do not like you and do not want to see you move ahead. People may even feel somewhat threatened by your qualifications or abilities. If you are going to climb the slippery heights of the career ladder, you need to keep your wits about you. Be aware of what's going on and the implications of participating. If you end up playing the 'game', then you possibly risk becoming like the power-hungry, politically-motivated types you are trying to avoid and losing your sense of honesty and integrity. Yet a degree of gamesmanship will be necessary to move forward.

In an ideal world, the boss would express pleasure with our work and offer us a well-deserved promotion, with everybody else standing around and applauding our good fortune. Unfortunately, in most organisations the reality is somewhat different. Once someone is promoted, the knives tend to come out, and quite pleasant staff members are transformed with envy. 'Why wasn't it me?' or 'Gary doesn't deserve that promotion, I've been here longer than he has ... ' or 'Why should Jenny get the new position and the new office. She was always the boss's favourite ... ' A delicate balance, like a spider's web, has been upset, rattled and shaken. You need to continue to be the same person you were before and rise above all of this. If you cannot continue any longer in such a company, if too many road blocks have been put in your way, you need to find an alternative position. Try for a transfer to another branch, or state, within the same company. But don't be fooled. Even if you work in a small company with a handful of staff, political manoeuvres and accusations can still occur. You need only two people to create conflict.

So, how do you combat this situation? If you choose to do nothing, you may have your progress impeded. If you play the game, you may end up impeding others. Climbing the ladder can be a long and treacherous journey with many pitfalls along the way. The idea is not to concentrate your energies so much on the ladder as on doing a job well and enriching your life and the lives of others in the process. If you spend all your time in political intrigue, you become a target for corporate and 'coffee-break' snipers. One honest way to make yourself 'grease-proof' is by dedicating yourself to the job at hand. But remain wary of the office 'politicians'. There will always be people within an organisation who will try to stop you and put obstacles in your way. But unless you work alone, be prepared for a potentially slippery ride.

50
Standing still or moving on
the mission statement check-up

Your mission statement is now twelve months old. You remember preparing it and thinking to yourself, 'I'm glad I did that. Now I can get on with my life without worrying too much about the mission statement.' You can do that, and of course your life will go on. But your mission statement is meant to be a living, flexible document, reflecting a whole range of things about you and your objectives. If you don't review it occasionally, the whole exercise may have been a waste of time.

As we said in chapter 20 on the mission statement, it is essential that the statement comes from within you and covers all aspects of your life, not simply your career or financial goals. If you prepared your mission statement carefully and honestly it's likely that, over time, it will become like an item of clothing that you periodically take out of the cupboard, wear, and then put back into the cupboard. You always know that it's there, what it's like and what it's for. So remember to review it regularly.

Standing still or moving on?

> ✯
> There is no need to judge yourself as good or bad, right or wrong. Simply review the progress and the setbacks and try to understand why things have turned out the way they have.

It is wise to conduct a formal review of your mission statement every twelve months to see how you've gone. What goals have you achieved? In what areas have you fallen short and why do you think this has happened? What have you learnt from preparing the mission statement and reviewing it? Look at the things that you could have done but didn't. Ask yourself why. If the objectives are still valid but haven't been achieved, what do you need to do?

This review can be enormously productive and positive. There is no need to judge yourself as good or bad, right or wrong. Simply review the progress and the setbacks and try to understand why things have turned out the way they have. You always need to move on from where you are now, not from some other place. Therefore, a better understanding of where you are now and how you arrived there is likely to help your planning for the next twelve months and beyond. Indeed, the more you understand, the more valuable the longer-term mission statement will be.

After some time, maybe even after a few years, you may notice that what you set down for yourself in your mission statement and what you actually achieve have moved closer together. But remember a couple of important points. Don't simply become a slave to your mission statement. You need to be flexible and not allow your mission statement to become just another crutch or security blanket. As we've said before, when exciting and unexpected opportunities arise, be prepared to examine and act on them even if they are outside the scope of your mission statement. The other point is if, after some time, you seem to be achieving everything you set for yourself, maybe you need to be a bit more adventurous, and set different or higher goals, if you feel that's appropriate.

Remember that it doesn't matter what you aspire to be or do, or how much in the way of material rewards you desire. It is still worthwhile having a regular check-up along the way. Just as a gardener watches a flower grow, or we take our car for a regular service, or ourselves to the doctor for a physical check-up, so it is well worth the effort to give our lives a regular check-up just to see if things are going according to plan. The mission statement is a productive starting point.

51
Job security
the myth

Let's get one thing straight. Job security is a myth. It doesn't exist any more. Nobody in a corner office is going to hand you a cosy, warm, secure position, so don't expect it. Many people take a particular job, or work in a certain field, not because they want to, but because they imagine it's 'secure'. It's secure until you are made redundant, or the firm is taken over, or the company simply goes out of business.

Many people work in government offices or large companies searching for the Holy Grail of security. They never find it. They spend a lifetime in anonymous, harshly-lit buildings, filing in and filing out every day. Even if they are never made redundant, they may still have paid a high price for their lifetime of security, something they realise only when it's too late. Many people appear to be in a constant state of fear about losing their jobs. They get so scared, their work suffers and it becomes a self-fulfilling prophecy. Eventually they do get the sack. When that happens they say 'I just knew it would happen ... '

People who are desperately seeking this security are also

> If you take away just one message from reading this book, make sure it's this one: nobody is going to give you security. You have to create your own.

denying themselves one of life's great pleasures—risk. If you take away just one message from reading this book, make sure it's this one: nobody is going to give you security. Like so many other things in life, you have to create your own sense of security. By creating your own inner security you need never be unemployed, or dependent on others; you learn to become 'fireproof', i.e. you can't be fired.

How does one achieve this seemingly impossible state of being? If you are very good at what you do, then there will always be a market for your services. Are you a good salesperson? Are you a terrific teacher? Are you a brilliant gardener, scientist or plumber? You have to understand that security isn't an automatic right or something that is imparted to you, like the teachings of an ancient sect. It's something you carry with you like a tortoise carries its shell. 'Have skills and experience, will travel'. You are your own security. When you enjoy your work, and hone your skills, you will have a sense of security because you will be secure about who you are and what you do. You won't need anybody else to confer security on you. If you are able to accept this responsibility, then a huge burden of fear will start to lift from your shoulders.

Your quest shifts its focus from merely craving security, to excelling at work, to being more adventurous and seeking more fulfilment from what you do. Funnily enough, this will actually create more security, because you just improve. You move from outer to inner security. Your thinking is no longer 'I hope I can keep this job for at least another year', but 'I'm enjoying the work, how can I make it even better ... ?' Craving security takes up a lot of our thinking time, time that could better be employed elsewhere. Once freed of the burden, you think more clearly; it's like opening a huge window in your mind.

External security is an illusion; it's something that's

JOB SECURITY

> ✬ Many people are, for a variety of reasons, scared to jump. It's only when they are pushed that they discover a whole new world.

promoted to keep people 'in their place', because their economic security is continually at stake. Permanent security can also be a curse. Just imagine for a moment that your boss tells you that you will not be sacked, ever, and that you will work with the same company for the rest of your life, with the same office, the same challenges. So what? What have you possibly gained? Quite the contrary; you've been robbed of an opportunity to grow, develop and discover your real strengths. Have you sold out? For a lot of people, the knowledge that they will work for the same company for the rest of their lives can be quite comforting. If that's what they genuinely want and it provides them with the level of fulfilment they seek, then its okay. Many people are, for a variety of reasons, scared to jump. It's only when they are pushed that they discover a whole new world out there, a world of danger sure, but also a world of undreamed-of opportunity.

The lure of being your own boss is hard to resist. Many are tempted but are reluctant to leave the shelter of a full-time job. The easiest thing in the world is to do nothing, not rock the boat. The money is coming in, the bills are being paid, what more could you want? Those who do their homework first and then decide to take the plunge often reap the benefits of flexible working hours, and the knowledge that they are working for themselves, not the boss down the corridor. If they need time off they don't have to ask anybody; they're answerable only to themselves. Their security comes from knowing that they are running the business well, taking care of finances, customer service and

JOB SECURITY

a host of other matters. No matter how tough the going gets, they have security because they do what they do well, and they have control over the business and their lives. They also have the capacity to shrink in harsh times, and expand in good times. It's another case of choices and consequences, and choosing to pay the price whether you desire employment or self-employment.

There *are* still a few jobs around that come with a measure of security. Top-ranking lecturers and professors are offered so-called 'tenure' which means they have that job for the rest of their working life, but even these positions are becoming much rarer and academia is certainly no longer a ticket to job security.

> Driving the engine is a lot more fun than being just a passenger on someone else's train ride.

For those who crave adventure, and would like to avoid boredom at all costs, security is lower down the priority list. As we said earlier, you have to create your own security. It's like laying down your own train tracks as you move forward. You determine the direction, and then begin to lay down the tracks. Sometimes you'll have to cross a gorge, or an arid desert, but at least you are moving forward, and you have control. It's your track, your adventure, no one else's. How good and committed you are at what you do will determine the length of the track and the direction you move in. Regardless of what happens, driving the engine is a lot more fun than being just a passenger on someone else's train ride.

52
Losing your job and other setbacks
opportunity knocks again

You are completely devastated! You have arrived at work and been called into the managing director's office to be told that the firm is 'downsizing'. Your services are no longer required. A million thoughts zip through your mind. You don't know what to do. How will you cope? Where will the next job come from? How will you pay the bills? You are scared and angry and don't know which way to turn or what to do. You always thought you had a secure job; you were a loyal employee and you assumed your company would always look after you. WRONG.

Of course, at the time and shortly thereafter, there is likely to be little joy in the harsh reality of losing your job. There

> ✡
> Now is the time to review how your life has been going and what you really want from it.

LOSING YOUR JOB AND OTHER SETBACKS

will be real pain, anger and devastation. Nevertheless, it is important to try to understand what has happened and see it as an important opportunity. Now is the time to review how your life has been going and what you really want from it. What are your priorities? Ironically, it is both an awful, yet perfect, time to do a mission statement check-up.

It is clearly very difficult to do this while undergoing a grieving process and make no mistake, losing your job involves a lot of grieving and pain. Why? Because the structures you have so carefully put in place over many years have, in a few brief moments, been blown away. Now you have to start to piece together the bits of a new, unknown, jigsaw puzzle. But first you must take a long, hard, honest look at your life and reflect on all aspects of it.

In our society we place a lot of emphasis on our working lives. Where, what, how and so on. Clearly, our careers generally provide us with much-needed meaning, status, money, social networks and so on. When we lose our job we appear to lose all these things. But we have not lost them forever. This is why it is critical to confront our basic life issues; not just because the unemployment queues are getting longer and staying that way, but because they are full of people who once had hope but now see their lives as hopeless and confused. We could ask whether the work structure that once provided so much stability has become the confining prison that prevents us from moving on. One of our most important resources (however buried it might appear to be) is our ability to understand ourselves (our needs and desires) and make the best use of our abilities. So what opportunities does job loss offer? What doors can it open?

1. You have the opportunity to create a space in your life: time out to think and contemplate.
2. You can take an open, honest look at yourself.

LOSING YOUR JOB AND OTHER SETBACKS

3. You can rebuild and re-evaluate your sense of self and your self-esteem.
4. To a degree, you can regain a sense of security. You know that the worst has happened. The fear and anticipation at least are gone.
5. You can re-examine some of your old notions and assumptions about your career options.
6. You can reflect on your priorities and develop a new strategy.
7. You can begin building a new structure for yourself. This is a new beginning. Define a new direction and set down a proper, solid foundation.
8. Break down the task into small manageable steps. Don't try to do too much at once.

> ✵
> Don't be daunted by the task. Change takes courage at the best of times.

By undertaking this process you can gradually begin to rebuild your life with new purpose. Purpose is a key concept because this is an opportunity to redefine your purpose. Will you continue in the same old way or will you use this opportunity as a catalyst to bring about radical change?

Don't be daunted by the task. Change takes courage at the best of times. In the midst of the turmoil caused by unemployment, courage may seem almost impossible. That's why you need your sense of purpose and mission: to give you the energy to move forward.

It doesn't matter in which area you start to rebuild; whether it's that course of study you always wanted to pursue, or the hobby you always felt you could make something of. Maybe it's the small business you wanted to start, or a new friendship or existing relationship you would really like to develop. All are equally legitimate if they come from within you. Any one of them could be the starting point of a new journey.

Once you start to walk down this new path, you might be quite surprised by how many wonderful things there are to enjoy. You might even feel just a touch thankful that you had the opportunities before it was too late to make these discoveries. It's not the end. It's another beginning.

53
Creating a balance
work to live or live to work

Have you ever met anybody who struck you as being totally driven by some deep need to be physically perfect, abundantly wealthy or, as is often the case, so possessed by their career that nothing else seemed to have any relevance or significance in their lives? The more they take on the more they need to take on.

Their seemingly obsessive pursuit of their chosen task becomes the means by which they choose to define themselves. This is not to say that ambition and determination are inherently bad or destructive. They are not, and in fact can be highly energising and enriching. With some people, however, the idea of achieving some balance, of having a rich inner life, or a deep spiritual life to provide some much needed and refreshing balance, seems to serve no useful purpose.

Take Dave: people who knew him could see he was totally driven by his ruthless, competitive determination to get to the top of his tree, no matter what the cost. His pursuit of the top job meant he had no time for 'non-

Creating a Balance

useful' friends, time-wasting small talk or worrying about his inner world. Even his family, who craved attention and affection, he found something of a burden.

For many years Dave's career appeared to be going along brilliantly. He worked incredibly hard to beat the competition, to ensure that he would get the top job. He played the politics beautifully in order to be the one in line for the job he most desired. Then a problem arose. About twelve months ago, Dave's firm was taken over by a large overseas company that preferred to put its own people in the top jobs. Within six months, Dave was redundant. He was forty-eight years old and felt he was on the scrap heap. He couldn't understand it—fifteen years with the same company. He thought he did everything right, played all the right games, made all the right noises and sacrificed everything. Indeed, he had nothing else in his life.

You see, along the way Dave had forgotten about his 'other lives'. Over the years he had forgotten about his emotional and spiritual needs, and how to integrate them with other aspects of his life. He had become so preoccupied with success that he didn't see the downside of what would be left if things didn't work out. Indeed, for Dave there was never any doubt, or allowance for things going wrong. For the first time he had to rebuild his life in a way totally foreign to him. In acknowledging his crisis he faced his ultimate reality as a human being with real emotional and spiritual needs. The single-minded pursuit of success that had driven him to extremes had failed to deliver in other critical areas of his life. He had been living only to work, not working to live. There had been no balance and no thought about the consequences of such a one-sided approach.

Soon, Dave had little choice but to explore his deeper needs and try to understand what they meant to him. For a while he tried to busy himself with a host of new outside activities. Some of these provided mental and intellectual stimulation but none really provided the focus to allow him to understand himself. It seemed that Dave had spent so long operating on the surface, that he had neglected and denied everything in his life that was going on underneath—his inner world. But at last, Dave realised that it was only by confronting and embracing his pain, his emptiness that he could start again to rebuild some true balance into his life. It was not too long before Dave started to work again, this time as a consultant to companies on business strategies, especially personal development strategies for senior executives. He had always considered this to be 'wishy washy' nonsense. Dave had always been a 'hard numbers 'n' facts' man, but not any more.

> ✯ His greatest mistake had been the imbalance he had created in his life and the enormous price he had paid.

In realising that his greatest mistake had been the imbalance he had created in his life and the enormous price he had paid, Dave was determined to bring his life back into some kind of balance. He began embracing a whole range of new activities which expanded his horizons and allowed him to explore new ideas and challenges; activities from which he could derive some meaning.

It had taken Dave a long time to accept that he was a complex person with strong feelings and emotional needs, and that he had to recognise and deal with these in his own way. Moreover, he accepted that his spiritual well-being demanded that he examine his innermost private life and come to terms with his own needs, while embracing his strengths as well as his limitations. In discovering his inner self, Dave discovered many other important things in his life—his family, friends, his desires and dreams. He had created a new life as well as an inner core of calm and peace that imparted a new sense of meaning.

For Dave, his experiences came late and at a very high cost. Now he is learning and teaching others the importance of recognising

Creating a Balance

the warning signs before it is too late. After much pain, Dave can now acknowledge that it's okay to be ambitious and single-minded, to pursue goals. However, it may not be okay to be compulsively possessed and obsessed by such pursuits, particularly if they end up controlling and ultimately destroying your life and failing to equip you with the inner strength and skills you need to face life.

In the normal humdrum of daily life it is so easy to skim over the surface and ignore what is happening at deeper levels, looking only at the immediate issues and problems at hand. But it may be that we could do more to enrich and balance our lives if we were able to recognise and embrace the significance, not only of our physical, but also of our mental and spiritual lives, and treat them all as equally important and deserving of our attention and affection.

It is possible to contrast Dave's lifestyle with that of someone who is preoccupied with developing the various aspects of themselves. In a sense, playing a musical instrument is a good example, because it brings your physical, mental and spiritual sides into balance. The physical side is your technical ability to play the instrument, to produce the right notes. The mental aspect is your musicianship, your ability to put the technique to work and to play the music in your own distinctive way. The spiritual aspect is different again. It is that almost indescribable ability that allows you to transform the notes and your interpretation into pure magic and artistry. It is the ability to tap the most hidden corridors of your inner self. Those areas that have been captivated by the music enable you and others to be transported to a higher plane, to produce a performance of lasting significance. The same can be true in any art form and even in sporting endeavours. That sense of magic combines the physical, mental and spiritual qualities. Helen understood this well.

Helen was an extremely gifted pianist. For years she practised hard and struggled to improve her technique. On several occasions she almost abandoned playing, frustrated by her lack of progress. But she didn't give up. She kept going and so continued to improve. As her technique improved, her ability to develop her musicianship emerged. As her sense of musicianship built, so did her confidence.

Although it took a while for her to realise it, Helen came to see that music was the medium by which all the things that really mattered in her life could be kept together and balanced. For the first time she felt comfortable with her ability to express herself through her music. Even though public performances were important, and she gave many, these were not the most important aspects. Helen now feels fortunate and grateful for the ability (Helen always says 'gift') to use music to bring together the various aspects of herself. Through her music she continues to develop a deeper understanding of herself.

The central issue is not that one type of lifestyle is better than another, but that we should recognise the importance of developing all the various aspects of ourselves and maintaining a sense of balance. It is as important to be passionate about our beliefs as it is to set goals for the achievement of our desires.

54
Mind and body
keeping both fit

As we've tried to demonstrate throughout this part of the book, no matter what you do for a living, no matter how hard you work or study, it's essential to have some balance in your life. If you are spending a lot of time indoors, if you are sitting around in traffic all day, you need to recognise the imbalance and do something about it.

The insights we look at in this book aren't purely about self-image, relationships, beliefs and other 'internal' areas: they're also about having a valuable 'external' life as well. You function in the real world, so part of life is about having a good time, enjoying sports, hobbies and spending time with family and friends. Not only is this okay, it's essential. Everyone has an enormous amount to contribute to relationships and friendships, so share yourself with those who are close to you. Go out there and enjoy all that life has to offer. Be a part of it, not just a spectator.

> Go out there and enjoy all that life has to offer. Be a part of it, not just a spectator.

It is important to balance your 'inner world' by developing a sense of real connection with the outside

MIND AND BODY

world. Go for a bike ride, fly a kite or have a picnic. If you maintain your physical health and fitness (you don't have to become an athlete), your mental health will similarly benefit. Exercise can make you feel better, more alert and less lethargic. From time to time, shift focus from the mental to the physical. That alone can be very refreshing. There is little point in having all the important skills that are discussed in this book if you are always feeling tired and run-down and have that 'can't be bothered' approach. Some physical toning up will certainly invigorate you and put a spring in your step.

In terms of keeping your mind fit, there is really no substitute for what you are doing now, reading. Reading is like gymnastics for the brain. Just look at the range of books and subjects available to you: science fiction, mystery, biography. Not only will reading keep your brain alert and ticking over, but you can also learn something, picking up extra knowledge that could change the way you look at life.

Jan is an accountant, and a very good one at that. She runs a thriving practice and is well liked by her clients and friends. The trouble with Jan is that she has little else beyond her narrow area of expertise. She hasn't read a novel since high school, and the only time she goes into bookshops is to buy stationery. She feels that she's missing out on something, but says that the weight of her work and reading in her area doesn't allow the luxury of general reading. Even so, Jan still manages to watch about twenty hours of TV a week, which is about three hours a night. If she halved her TV viewing and read a book (any book except accounting!), she would be adding some value to her life. Too much TV isn't life-enhancing; in fact it subtracts from your life. Your brain goes into neutral and the TV attempts to entertain you. Reading requires you to work and think more, but the rewards are tremendous.

MIND AND BODY

Are you like Jan? Is your day so full that you don't have time, or can't make time available, to read? If you take public transport to work or school or university, you can use that time to read instead of staring out of the bus or train window. The window frame is simply another sort of TV screen, isn't it? Remember, this is the only life you have, so why not try to enhance it as much as possible, whenever possible?

You really cannot begin to become master of your life skills until you are prepared to take a more balanced approach to your life. Look at it as a whole. A balanced life is more than just your emotional behaviour and responses. It's also what you eat, what exercise you get, how much enjoyment you give and get throughout the day and a lot of other factors. Keeping both mind and body fit requires effort and dedication. They affect each other, so start NOW, even if it means putting this book down and going for a walk around the block. It may be your first step to leading a more balanced, productive and integrated life.

55
Humour and other escape valves

Have you ever been inside a boiler room in a factory or ship? Steam is building up and the needle on the pressure gauge is almost touching the red line. People are running around all over the room checking the boilers. Everywhere you look there is tension. And then all of a sudden somebody releases a valve and there is a great rush as the steam escapes and the needle in the pressure gauge falls back to normal. The scene is one that in many ways resembles our own lives. We race around undertaking a million and one tasks and over-committing ourselves. Even if we feel that we are under-utilised, the same result may be produced. The pressure keeps on rising and rising until we either explode or we activate one of our own release valves.

Learning to develop an appropriate release valve (or more than one) and knowing when to hit it can be a tremendously useful and important skill, because it can, in a very practical way, act as a catalyst for many of the other skills discussed throughout this book. Your release valve can take almost any shape or form you choose so long as it

Humour and other escape valves

diffuses the chaos, pressure and anxiety in your daily life. It can introduce balance and provide the opportunity to reflect on some of the issues that daily pressures seldom allow you to consider.

Les and Rosa had been living together for several years and had both developed pretty hectic lifestyles. Rosa worked as a research scientist and Les as a journalist. They were used to working long hours and in the early days together used to bring all their tensions and frustrations home and dump them on each other. After a while they realised that their lives had developed a monotonous routine and their anxieties were not helping the relationship. They recognised the need to throw themselves into some other activities in order to channel their energies and relieve their stress. As a younger man Les had been a rather good saxophonist. So he decided to form a small jazz group with a few of his old friends. Twelve months later the group is still meeting and practising one night a week. Occasionally they do a gig or two at a local club. Les loves it.

Rosa always enjoyed telling jokes and acting. Six months ago she decided to put together some of her favourite routines. After getting a positive response from a few friends, she worked up the courage to try out in a nightclub. She got a job performing two nights a week and she's having a ball. She can't think of a better escape valve than humour. It's not only a total contrast to what she does during the day, but the pleasure Rosa gets from standing up in front of an audience and making the guests laugh just radiates from her face. Not only that, it enables her to tackle her other work with renewed enthusiasm, having got rid of the tension and anxiety that she found so debilitating. Ever since Rosa had been a small girl, humour had been her favourite escape; now it was of even more use and pleasure to her and to others.

Humour and other escape valves

> ✵ If you constantly feel like blowing your stack you are desperately in need of finding an escape valve.

It doesn't matter if your release valve is humour or something else. It can be anything you enjoy, like reading, bushwalking, cycling, tennis, pottery, painting or gardening. They are all equally useful if they help you to relax and enjoy life while allowing you to let off steam and create a feeling of peace, balance and integration in your life, not to mention the health benefits of releasing stress and tension.

If you constantly feel like blowing your stack and spend the greater part of your life feeling totally stressed out, screaming at people, unable to think clearly, with no peace of mind, then you are desperately in need of finding an escape valve—sooner rather than later. When you know the difference such a release can make to the quality of your life and the pleasure it can bring, you will wonder why it took so long to find it. The related benefits in helping to keep your mind and body fit, as well as bringing all aspects of your life together, cannot be under-estimated.

56
The power of creativity and imagination

Where would we be without imagination? Imagination is the fuel that feeds our desires, our hopes, our dreams, our goals. How often have you heard people say that they lack imagination, or aren't 'creative'? Everybody is creative to some degree. You may not be a brilliant composer, or an artist, but you are still creative. Have you ever made up a joke? Have you ever said something funny at a party or a meeting? Have you ever wished that you could do something different from, or better than the way you are doing things at the moment? Well, the good news is that you *are* creative. You *have* the imagination to think of these things.

> The good news is that you *are* creative.

It's very easy to say that you are not particularly creative. How do you know unless you actually give your creativity the opportunity to blossom? Unless you try your hand at dancing and dancing lessons how do you know you can't dance? Unless you pick up a paint-brush, how do you know you can't paint?

THE POWER OF CREATIVITY AND IMAGINATION

Estelle liked collecting ceramics, little glazed pots and jugs. Some were round with perfectly shaped lids that made them look like spheres that could be split in two. She loved the textures that could be achieved with varying glazes and firing techniques. Whenever there was a ceramics exhibition at a gallery, Estelle would be there marvelling at the incredible shapes, colours and textures.

Over coffee one day, a friend of Estelle's suggested that she should try her hand at creating some of her own pottery and ceramics. Estelle laughed. What a preposterous thought; she wasn't an artist, she couldn't create anything like that. Her friend simply said, 'But have you tried?' It suddenly occurred to Estelle that although she loved the ceramics, she had never even thought about creating her own. Her first excuse was 'I haven't got the time.' Do you know what her friend said? 'Make the time.'

Over the next few weeks, she thought about attending a ceramics course. She thought about all the pros and cons. Despite initial misgivings and hesitation, she enrolled. It was one night a week for eight weeks. Her first attempts were a complete disaster. Nothing worked. She could work with the shapes, but when they were ready to be fired in the kiln, they would crack or shatter. But Estelle didn't give up. She continued learning, and enrolling in courses. She was really enjoying herself. Within about two years, friends started buying items of ceramics from her: salt and pepper shakers, a fruit bowl, a set of glazed mugs. Last year, Estelle, along with other artists in her area, held a small exhibition of work at the local town hall. All of Estelle's work was sold.

> What about exercising the 'imagination muscle'?

Estelle channelled her imagination, fantasy and desire into a positive outcome. She became what she never thought she could

The Power of Creativity and Imagination

become, an artist. She had the courage to follow through, to persevere, but she also used her creativity and imagination.

We put a lot of effort into physical fitness, and that's great. But what about exercising the 'imagination muscle'? Like a muscle, the more you use your imagination, the better it will work for you. On a very practical and pragmatic level, your imagination will help you see possibilities, choices and options. It may be the key to embracing your desires and finding real purpose and meaning in your life. How many people do you know who have made unfortunate choices in their lives, because they lacked the imagination to see the outcome? It's almost like having a video player in your mind that you set on fast-forward to glimpse a future outcome. They borrowed too much money to buy a car—they lacked the imagination to see the consequences of the debt. They hurt someone's feelings—they lacked the imagination to see the consequence of what they said or did. Not having the capacity to think ahead, and not using your imagination can get you into trouble. 'If I do this, can I imagine what the possible outcome will be?'

There is one absolutely beautiful thing about imagination. It's private. You don't have to share it with anybody. It's just you and your mind quietly running through imagined options and outcomes. It's almost like flicking through a series of postcards or video movies to see which ones appeal to you. In the privacy of your own mind you can sort and sift through the information. There is nothing to be embarrassed about because nobody else is listening. It's a powerful tool that can be used to deal with your emotions.

There are a number of ways to stimulate your imagination. One of the best ways is reading books. It really doesn't matter whether it's science-fiction, biography, crime stories, anything. Books can help you create a 'theatre of the

THE POWER OF CREATIVITY AND IMAGINATION

mind'. All the action takes place inside your head. You must have heard people say after a film that 'it's not as good as the book'. No studio or director can come up with the sort of fantastic images that you can conjure up in your own mind. Here's an example. 'The pilot was at the controls of the damaged jet fighter, but something was wrong. Frantically he tried to pull the plane out of the dive. He radioed ahead for help; he was now only minutes from smashing into the ocean. He had one last chance; he hit the red ejector-seat button hard, the canopy flew off, and he shot out of the spinning jet. His bright yellow chute opened, just as his plane crashed into the water, sinking without a trace.' Well, did you see the action in your 'mind's eye'? Everyone would have imagined the action from a different angle, with different elements, but the action and the tension would have been the same.

Reading books will stimulate your imagination, and take you to undreamed-of worlds, where you'll meet some fascinating characters. Think about integrating the power of your imagination into your daily life. It can enrich your life in ways you probably can't even imagine ... yet!

Part 6

Financial security or insecurity

57
Money
handle with care

Money, like a potion that promises eternal youth, can be both a blessing and a curse. It can help you in various ways or it can overwhelm you in a way that ultimately may destroy relationships, careers, and eventually yourself. What is it about money that makes it such a potentially dangerous commodity that it should be marked 'Handle With Care'? The difference is all to do with how we choose to view money and the importance or significance we give it in our lives.

Clearly, having money allows us to do all sorts of things. It can underpin a quality (and quantity) of life that otherwise you could only dream of. Money can open doors, deliver power, influence and status. It can be a great tool, a common language that everyone, everywhere seems to understand and is more than a little interested in.

But it can also be a curse. Unless you recognise and understand the power of money, it can control you, by influencing your decisions and actions, by impacting on your behaviour, by reducing everything in your life to a judgement about the importance of money. Decisions are based purely on the monetary value of something. Human or emotional aspects of decisions are often disregarded. All your actions will be motivated by the desire for more and more money just for the sake of it.

Perhaps money already has this impact on your life. You

> Money alone can never fill the inner void.

may have adopted a certain lifestyle that demands a certain level of income. It seems essential (and logical) to maintain that lifestyle and in so doing the need for money, more money, traps you. You have become a prisoner of the money curse: its allure is likely to keep you in this position for a considerable period, perhaps forever.

If you are serious about breaking the money curse, you must first be prepared to recognise and accept money's addictive qualities. You must also be able to recognise that regardless of your current lifestyle, your bank balance will never be big enough. As the amount of money you have increases, so do your needs and wants. One feeds off the other, always directed towards the outer world and material needs, trying to fill an inner void. Money alone can never fill the inner void. By re-examining our overall priorities, we begin to place the importance of money into a healthier perspective.

Does money still have to be handled with care if you don't have much? Of course it does. It's when your reserves are low that you have to be especially careful: this is when you can fall into a debt trap, and borrow too much. You may start to live beyond your means, using credit cards as if they never have to be paid off. Handling any amount of money is a responsibility. When we don't have much, we want some; when we have money, we want more; there never seems to be enough.

In learning to handle money with care, it is important to remember that money can never replace what is inside us, our feelings and sense of integrity. By understanding what motivates us and by trying to keep the issue of money in perspective, we will learn to respect and handle money wisely. Part of this is understanding debt and borrowing. This is where people get into the most trouble. Using 'OPM', Other People's Money, especially a bank's money, is a big responsibility.

During the 1990s, after the excesses of the 80s, there has been a fundamental shift in attitudes about borrowing money and dealing with debt. Many people have reviewed their priorities and adopted a lower-key lifestyle, partly because many just can't afford anything else. We are much more cynical about wealth and its trappings, and less likely to admire it for its own sake. If we see someone in a flashy car, we now tend to say 'Must be in debt' or 'I wonder what the monthly repayments are'. A different set of values is replacing the 1980s race to accumulate the biggest and the best. It's critical that the lessons of the 80s be learnt so that the debts don't return, even if the good times do. So how do you keep the 'D' word under control? How do you ensure that you control debt, without the debt controlling you?

It's really a case of 'enter at your own risk'. Avoid getting into excessive debt in the first place. Debt can be helpful: there are times when we do need to borrow, for example to buy our first home or apartment. That debt has a different name. It's called a 'mortgage'. Keep in mind that the first four letters, 'mort', mean 'death' in French. We need to ensure that our debts don't become the death of us. When we pay 'interest' on a loan, we tend to forget that it is a debt. We call it a 'loan'. If we think of the interest we pay as rental for the money we borrow, we may be less inclined to borrow. For example, if you borrow $10 000 for twelve months at an interest rate of 5%, you have rented that money for $500. You still have to repay the $10 000. That $500 'rental' is pure income to the bank. That's one of the ways the bank makes its money.

The same approach applies to business. Many people just starting out think about leasing equipment. That's okay, as long as you are aware of your liabilities. Some people tend to think that the new equipment will cost only $450 a month; surely they can afford that. What they often fail to take into account are the other three pieces of equipment they are already leasing. Their monthly lease payments already total over $1500, plus the $450, that may be enough to tip them into the red. These payments have to be made whether the business is producing income or not.

Debt has another sinister way of controlling your life. It can force you to stay in a job you don't like. It can be a trap limiting your choices. Carrying debts can be like lugging around an enormous burden that you can't get rid of, thus creating more anxieties. Credit cards are also an easy trap for the unwary. Ideally, pay credit card bills in full when they fall due. You compound the problem by carrying debt over from one month to another. Sure, they're called 'credit cards', but until you pay them off they're really 'debt cards'. Some people even pay one credit card off with another. This is a shortcut to financial disaster. The sooner you realise that a credit card account does have to be paid, that the goods aren't free, the more responsible you're likely to be. If you can't afford to pay credit card bills then you are overspending. If you get into trouble, there are financial counsellors who can help you identify problems and suggest ways to improve your situation.

If you can pay for something in cash, do so. Avoid borrowing if you can. If you must borrow, do so responsibly and make sure you can afford the repayments. Don't be talked into borrowing more than you need.

Getting into debt is often a source of surprise and mystery to many people. They think it happened almost by accident. Without financial plans, budgets or goals, things can go off the rails. You must take responsibility for every level of your life. Your financial well-being is as important as your emotional and spiritual well-being: they affect each other in many ways. Think of the action and the consequences, and make sure you can live with the result.

58
Status and wealth

Status and wealth. What are they? Why do so many people covet them? Why are many people willing to cheat, lie and kill for them? What happens once you have achieved your desired level of status and wealth?

Status is about our real or perceived position in society. Depending on your politics, the country you live in, status is a flexible and illusory thing. If a dictator grabs power, they are perceived to have status; if a politician becomes a president or prime minister, then they have status. If you become the chairman of a group of companies, you have status of a sort. Artists, musicians and writers can have status conferred upon them. An Academy Award confers status on the recipient. As you can see, status has many facets and is as real as you want to make it.

Status symbols are used to reflect that status: a big house, an expensive car, a business jet, expensive clothes and jewellery. These all reflect the real or perceived status of the owner. We say 'perceived' because status exists in the minds of the beholder and the person to whom we direct that perception. We can choose to respect that person, say, a millionaire business person, because we are impressed with what they have done. Or we can choose not to be impressed and simply say, 'So what?' Not everybody reacts to status in the same way. Status is like a currency that can be traded

Status and Wealth

and exchanged for various goods and services, as long as people believe in the status.

Wealth is often, though not always, attached to status. People like to believe that money confers some sort of status automatically. Are we impressed by wealthy people because of who they are or because of what they have?

Many people pay a terrible price for status and wealth. Rock stars have paid with their lives: wars have been fought, crimes have been committed, people have put themselves and their families through personal anguish. For what? Has the price been worth it? It rarely is. We made the point in chapter 10 that you can spend years trying to climb that mountain, then wonder what all the fuss was about once you got there. You're still you, warts and all. People are often bitterly disappointed. The wealth and status may change you. It can go to your head, and your family and friends may long for the return of the person they used to know.

In a society like ours, many of us tend to place a lot of value on status and the money that sometimes goes with it. We judge films by how much money they make, and the awards they have won ... the status of the film. We judge cars by their price and where they were made ... the status of the automobile. We feel insecure unless something or somebody has some sort of stamp or seal of approval. The restaurant must have some sort of ranking or grading. The clothes we wear: do they have some sort of 'cult status' that makes them desirable? It's everywhere we look.

> ✵
> Inner wealth and inner tranquillity, coupled with good health, will give you all the riches you really need.

We need to be able to cut through all these perceptions and see things as they really are. We'd like to point out that not all status or wealth is bad. The question is, how did you achieve them and what do you do with them now?

Inner wealth and inner tranquillity, coupled with good health, will give you all the riches you really need. If you cultivate your inner wealth and your inner spirit, you will have less of a need to impress and to accumulate outer trappings. When somebody's wealth comes from within, external trappings become irrelevant. Their wealth comes from integrity and finding joy in the work they do and the balanced life they lead. They may also have financial wealth; but it is not a consuming passion and it is not there to impress others. They may be content to live a modest existence and share their wealth with others less fortunate.

Continue reading in this subject area; find out about the benefits of inner wealth. The rewards in health and tranquillity will far outweigh anything you can place in a bank account.

59
Needs and wants
what's the difference?

Our needs are really very simple. We need food, shelter and clothing. With these bare essentials we can get by. With a roof over our heads we are protected from the elements. With food in our stomachs we are not hungry. With clothing we are not cold. These are basic human needs.

However, many of us go way, way beyond these basic needs, to the next level known as 'wants'. There are lots of things we want that we don't really need. We can survive without television. We don't really need the latest pair of jeans, or the latest whiz-bang gadget. We still want these things for all sorts of reasons. The wealthier you are, the smaller the gap between what you need and what you want. In fact the two become virtually indistinguishable. You may need a new car, but you want a Ferrari ... so you buy one. The less well-off you are, the greater the gap between what you need and what you want. You may have the basics, but that exotic car or overseas holiday may be way out of your reach. In this instance 'needs' and 'wants' are quite distinct.

It's important to be clear about the distinction between the two. Every time a new gadget or a fashion item arrives

NEEDS AND WANTS

we are tempted to say 'I need it', whereas what we really mean is 'I want it ... '

Nick is just like that. He has a perfectly good computer. It's fast, it's efficient, it's problem-free. But Nick has heard that there is a new model coming out. The new model looks slightly fancier, and is probably a fraction faster, but otherwise it's the same computer with a cosmetic 'face-lift'. The replacement computer is going to cost a lot of money. Nick's brother, Roger, tried to talk him out of it. All Nick could say was 'Don't you understand, I need a new computer ... ' Roger told him that there was nothing wrong with the computer he had; there was no real advantage in buying a new computer. Eventually Nick did buy the new computer. It was only new for about eight weeks, then it was superseded by an even faster, sleeker model that was actually cheaper!

Nick was blind to the difference between 'need' and 'want'. Most of the things we spend money on are things that we want. They make our lives more pleasant and we get a lot of enjoyment out of them. Although we don't need bikes, hi-fi equipment and sneakers, we still buy them, and there is nothing wrong with that, if we have the money. Our consumer society would probably collapse if people rationalised their purchases and bought only what they needed. The trouble comes with over-spending on 'wants'. We can end up in a debt spiral, borrowing money to pay off debts, and then creating another debt, each solution creating another problem.

> ✯
> Our consumer society would probably collapse if people rationalised their purchases and bought only what they needed.

Needs and Wants

There is a lot of pressure on us to buy and consume, so it's important to keep our needs and wants in some sort of perspective. We try to 'keep up with the Joneses', we need to look the part, it's a competitive world and the one with the most toys wins ... or is it? Sure, you're entitled to a treat now and again, and nobody expects you to walk around in worn-out shabby clothes. But don't give in to constant purchasing, and constant 'cruising' around shopping malls.

> It's what's inside your mind that counts, not what's inside your cupboards.

So often we buy things in an effort to satisfy some other underlying need.

We may be lonely or depressed, or would just like some cheering-up. Buying something makes us feel better for a while. But after you've left the shop clutching a bag of new clothes or whatever, what has really changed? Nothing. In fact, things may have worsened because now you've bought something you probably couldn't afford, and your credit card limit is at breaking point already.

The shopping expedition exacerbates the problem rather than fixing it. If you are going to buy something to make you feel better, simply set yourself a budget. Keep it low, because whether you buy something for $1000, $100, $50 or even less, the 'high' is still the same, so you may as well minimise the financial damage. Again, if you can, try to analyse and treat the inner cause of your problem, rather than mask it with a 'quick-fix' purchase. You'll need discipline to avoid spending and you'll need the capacity to think twice before reaching for your purse or wallet.

Beware of surrounding yourself with objects and using them as a way of assessing, defining or confirming your success or well-being. It's what's inside your mind that

NEEDS AND WANTS

counts, not what's inside your cupboards, in your garage or on your shelves.

'Needs' and 'wants' aren't simply the province of consumer spending. They can apply equally to relationships, careers, outside interests and status. You don't always need what you want, and you don't always want what you need. Keep things in balance; be in control and aware of your wants and needs. You'll save yourself a lot of stress and heartache if you keep the distinction clear, and think before you buy.

60
Spend now or spend later?

It's really quite amazing what you can buy these days—just about anything! Have you wandered into a department store recently? It seems that what you can't buy isn't worth having.

You have probably noticed that some of your friends have become 'consumer junkies', they just keep on buying things; it's terrific! Consumer junkies typically wait for the next gadget. When it arrives on the market, they're out to buy it as soon as it hits the shelf. Then, when the next model comes out—wham! Overnight the old model is no good and they just *have* to have the new one.

> Consumer junkies typically wait for the next gadget. When it arrives on the market, they're out to buy it.

As we have already seen, it's okay to consume if you really need to, but you don't have to. There are other things you can do with money. You can spend it, you can save it, you can invest it, you can even give it away. You can have a lot of fun with a dollar, but the problem is that once you've had your fun doing whatever you want, it's gone. Most of the things you do with a dollar result in you having less than a dollar left ... except in the case of investing.

Spend now or spend later?

One of the difficulties some people have with investing is that generally, it is quite boring. Nothing much seems to happen. You hand your money and instructions to the bank or your financial adviser and that's it! You don't go home with a product such as a video-cassette recorder, or a car. There's no excellent restaurant meal ... well, not immediately anyway. You invest the dollar and that's the last you see of it for maybe five or ten years. It's pretty boring and dull and most people just don't like doing it ... so they avoid it.

Jack and Mike are two people who have very different views on what they should do with their dollars. It seems that about five years ago, both had about $1000 spare cash. Jack was always very keen on filling his house with the latest gadgets and doing whatever he could to impress his friends with the latest 'toys'. Mike, however, was a little more cautious and while he enjoyed his creature comforts, he also saw the value of putting some money away.

About a month ago we received an update on what happened to Jack and Mike and their $2000. You wouldn't believe it. Jack is totally 'consumed out'. He has so many gadgets around him that he doesn't know what to do with them. In fact, he spent the same $1000 about ten times and now owes the bank so much money he doesn't quite know how he's going to meet his repayments. Mike made some investments in the stock market and his original $1000 is now worth nearly $7000. He sold his original investment and, after taking some advice, made further investments that have continued to perform well. He reinvested the profits from his original investment and this has served him very well. He regularly monitors his investments, and is not concerned that he's not out there spending.

Both Jack and Mike still seem content with the original

SPEND NOW OR SPEND LATER?

decisions they made. As we said, it's okay to invest and it's okay to consume. But if you want to determine what suits you, you have to determine your longer-term priorities. Too much consumption may use up investment funds and then they're gone for good. Think about how you're going to create the wealth necessary to achieve all your goals, based on the amount of money you have available. It's always your choice.

61
Savings
a regular habit

Saving money is a habit, just like spending. So many people go from week to week, pay-packet to pay-packet, spending every cent they earn. The same people also complain that they never have any spare cash when they need it. Yet they are responsible for their own spending and consumption.

> ✯ Take a few minutes to work out where your money goes.

Take a few minutes to work out where your money goes. Let's look at a simple but effective example. Do you buy lunch every day? Let's say you spend $6 a day on lunch: that's $30 a week which is roughly $1500 a year. All those seemingly insignificant $6 lunches do add up. If you only buy lunch three days a week, then at the end of the year you've saved $600. That could be a new TV set, or go towards a holiday. Perhaps more appropriately, it could be saved or invested and you have hardly inconvenienced yourself in the process.

Jan worked in an office block that had a coffee shop on the ground floor. The coffee shop made terrific cappuccinos. Twice a day Jan would take the elevator down to the shop and buy a coffee for $2; she sometimes even bought one for a friend who worked in the same department. These daily purchases were over and above what she spent on her lunch every day; that was about $6.50. Her daily food bill at work was around $10.50. That's $210 a month! Jan was also a bit of a spendthrift. She'd see something she liked and buy it. She would usually put it on a credit card and 'worry about it later'.

Her bills eventually mounted up. In despair she went to see a financial counsellor to sort out the mess. After finding out details about Jan's spending habits, the counsellor's first piece of advice was to 'drink instant coffee'. Jan didn't understand. The counsellor pointed out to a stunned Jan that she was spending $80 a month on cappuccinos, or roughly $960 a year, just on frothy cups of coffee! Jan gradually changed her habits, but it took a while, and she had to suffer being mocked by friends. She now thinks twice before she reaches for her purse. Gradually, she came to understand the difference between wants and needs, and the importance of financial planning and saving.

The savings habit is a key ingredient in achieving a level of financial security. The sooner you start the habit the easier it will become. You don't have to become a miser, hoarding money for its own sake. But savings can be an important tool to help you achieve a certain quality of life. You need to look beyond instant gratification, and feel a sense of accomplishment by saving for something that you really want.

By going without a few indulgences, and putting that money away, you are well on the way to paying for the house or apartment, or the new car or hi-fi gear, without going into debt. The pervading mentality of earlier generations was, 'If you can't afford it, don't buy it', 'Don't live beyond your means', and 'If you

> ✴ What is wrong with not buying something because you can't afford it?

SAVINGS

want something, save up and buy it'. While these seem like 'old fashioned' values it makes sense to go back to basics. What is wrong with *not* buying something because you can't afford it? It's easy to think that you need a new car. You go to a bank and take out a personal loan at a ridiculous interest rate. Easy. You don't think of the debt, or the implications of what that car really cost in total. Every month you have this debt hanging over you. You justify the purchase by saying it is a tax deduction. Could you have bought a cheaper car? Could you have saved up part of the funds, and only borrowed a portion of the cost? The bank will be happy until you fall behind in your repayments: then see what happens. See how free you are and how much you like your car!

We can develop helpful habits like savings and restraint or unhelpful habits such as over-spending. Once you have the habit of saving, you can set yourself savings targets, even just a few hundred dollars. Making a start is essential; after that it becomes easier. You'll come to regard savings as another form of spending, except you are spending your money on saving.

If you need further advice, then seek it out; but make a start. Open an account at a bank, and start accumulating some funds. Once you get into the savings habit you'll be well on your way to becoming financially smarter and independent.

62
Financial planning and budgeting
does it work?

Have you ever compared tackling two important tasks, one of which was planned while the other was totally unplanned? What were the outcomes for the planned activity as opposed to the one which was not planned? Similarly, have you ever set yourself certain objectives but have randomly gone about trying to achieve them and in the end achieved nothing at all? Finally, have you ever really wanted to buy something important but, because you thought you were never going to be able to afford it, you didn't even try to save for it? Does the same old negative thinking always appear to hold you back?

One of the first things to do in any personal financial plan is to work out how badly you want something, whether it be a car, a house, clothes, a holiday, an investment portfolio, a business: it doesn't matter what. Do you desire it so badly that you are prepared to change your whole way of thinking and acting in order to achieve it? If you are prepared to, then you are starting to be serious and this is where planning and budgeting come into play.

FINANCIAL PLANNING AND BUDGETING

If you are not used to these concepts they may well seem like a foreign language, and like all foreign languages the rules can take some time to learn. Patience, discipline and determination are essential.

Once you have decided what you want and how badly you want it, you can begin to visualise your objective being achieved. Then you can break down the path to your objective into small, manageable stages that become little markers against which to track your progress. If necessary, seek professional advice. There are plenty of financial advisers around.

Michael recently started his first job and really wanted to go overseas. He knew that it would cost a lot of money and he didn't know how he was going to get it. He had never saved seriously in his life. He had only spent seriously—all his money. But he had recently read that if he wanted to achieve a measure of financial control and discipline, he had to take seriously the responsibility to start planning and budgeting. It was no longer possible to continue his normal freewheeling spending and have an overseas trip. He began to think of saving as a form of deferred spending, like spending money on saving.

It wasn't going to be easy. He really had to establish the overseas trip as a goal and visualise stepping onto the plane, actually making it happen. Michael was determined, so he began by drawing up a detailed list of all his expenditure and income. He started to analyse carefully all those things he had to buy and those things he was prepared to go without. The importance of the trip would reflect how much he was prepared to shave from his budget. He also started to look carefully at his income to determine any ways to increase it. Could he take on extra work? Did he have any other special skills or experience from which he could earn additional income?

FINANCIAL PLANNING AND BUDGETING

By going through this process Michael determined how much he needed to save each week to achieve his goal. If the figures showed there was no surplus, he would have to cut back on his spending. He prepared what he considered to be a realistic plan with achievable targets. But he also gave himself the benefit of rewards. Each time he achieved one of his targets within the set time frame he would treat himself to a small reward. Twelve months and two weeks to the day, Michael went out and purchased his aeroplane ticket. He is currently overseas.

Michael is firmly of the view that without his careful planning and determination and, more importantly, without the radical shift in his attitudes to financial planning, he would not be travelling.

We can all embrace this concept if we really want to improve our financial position. However, we must be prepared to take responsibility for setting our own financial objectives and seeing them through to fruition. The task may be very difficult. There are likely to be all sorts of setbacks and problems along the way. But these are not as bad as endlessly making excuses and failing to set objectives. Simply spending our lives complaining that we never have sufficient money to do the things we want is a futile exercise.

> Simply spending our lives complaining that we never have sufficient money to do the things we want is a futile exercise.

The financial planning process begins with wanting badly enough to achieve something. It requires a plan based on a realistic assessment of income and expenditure and then the ability to visualise yourself achieving the goal. Rewarding yourself along the way for small achievements is as important as allowing yourself to make mistakes, because it is in the making of mistakes and learning from them that

FINANCIAL PLANNING AND BUDGETING

we improve our understanding and ability to plan and realistically secure our financial future.

Financial planning and budgeting does work. It's just hard work. You have to really want something and have a greater measure of financial control over your life. Work at your goals and keep an eye on your spending. It will pay you real dividends.

Part 7

Change and empowerment

63
Taking control of your life
the choices are yours

We saw in Part one how our life is so often concerned with making choices and taking responsibility for them as well as accepting their consequences. Making choices is also about assuming greater control over our life: making things happen instead of just letting them happen. Our choices shape our lives. They can either fill us with vitality and push us forward or sometimes destroy us.

It's very difficult to be in total control of your life. There are so many variables. You may feel that you are in control at work, but one day you discover that your office is moving interstate. You may get ill, you may arrive late at a crucial meeting ... a lot of things can and do happen along the way and

> Have a look at the things in your life that are working, as well as the things that aren't.

that's part of life. You need to be able to maximise your own potential and that's what we mean by taking control.

Taking control of your life

Maximising your potential involves taking a long hard look at yourself, and tapping into your real passions and working with them. This process should not involve any radical change. You need to take each step slowly. Have a good look at the things in your life that are working, as well as the things that aren't. Why are those parts of your life working for you? Why aren't others? You'll need to add a healthy dose of reality to your thinking as well. Maximising your potential doesn't mean thinking that you can be a rock star, quit your job and head for Los Angeles. One step at a time.

> The key to keeping control and maximising potential is developing the ability to tune out from the exterior noise and listen to the inner self.

A small step you can take is trying to be a little more assertive. Again, there are degrees. You don't need to become an outright tyrant, but less of a victim in those cases where you feel lacking in control. Many people are reluctant to say 'no' to a friend, relative or even a complete stranger. If you feel that you are being used, then try saying 'no'. This simple act of assertiveness can set you on the path to greater control. But think about this: saying 'yes' can do the same, because you can be assertive and say 'yes' as well. It just depends on the circumstances.

Do you have any habits that you would like to break? Now is the time. Do you smoke? Do you drink? Breaking old habits (especially bad ones) is a healthy step to regaining control. If you have some sort of addiction, however minor, then you are at the mercy of that habit: you are a victim of your own addiction. Just breaking a habit, though initially it may be extremely difficult, is an excellent start to reclaiming parts of yourself.

TAKING CONTROL OF YOUR LIFE

The key to keeping control and maximising potential is developing the ability to tune out from the exterior noise and listen to the inner self. Awareness of the inner self is a much better indicator of how much control we have over our lives. What are your inner voices saying to you about the person you are, the person you can be? Do you feel that you can do more, or less? Are you short-changing your life at the moment by accepting less and knowing that you are capable of getting more out of your life? What steps do you need to take to achieve this? How can you maximise your current situation and take advantage of current opportunities? Take some time to think about these and related issues.

In the context of living and functioning in society, you have the responsibility for making your own choices, determining your destiny and creating your own life. You can choose to change and improve, or do nothing. It is vital that you understand the significance of this, whether it be in dealing with change in your life, relationships, or career. If you are determined to assume greater control and responsibility, you will find that, rather than having fewer choices, you are likely to have more.

Having decided to take greater control, your actions and subsequent choices must be consistent. There is little point in choosing to be in control and acquire a deeper self-understanding if you then act as though it's not that important, or expect it to happen by magic. There is no instant magic—only the magic that will result from the inner and outer consistency of behaviour that you display. Taking responsibility for your own life empowers you to become your own agent for bringing about change and growth in your life.

If the changes that we bring about in our own lives inspire others to seek changes in theirs, in a sense we have empowered others.

Taking control of your life

If you really want to maximise your potential then you not only have to desire change but you have to be prepared to make changes—some large, some small. Some changes may appear small but may end up being quite profound. Remember: they are the result of your choices and ultimately your desire to determine the direction of your life.

If our mind-set is one that accepts change as normal and desirable, we are more likely to cope with it and to treat change as the heartbeat and rhythm of our lives.

64

The Near Life Experience

Most of us have probably heard a lot of talk about 'NDE's'. You know, Near Death Experiences, where people die for a few moments then miraculously snap back to life, and are able to remember the experience of 'dying' for the rest of their lives. Well, there is a new twist to that: we call it an 'NLE' or a Near Life Experience.

An NLE is very common, much more so than the NDE. Many of us are very busy every day with work, family, friends or coping with ill-health, travel and crises that crop up now and again. We are just too busy to inject some extra quality and 'time out' in our lives. When your whole life is a Near Life Experience, simply swept along by the hustle and bustle, you rob yourself of opportunities and adventures as well as a lot of happiness and satisfaction: not just you personally, but your whole family.

Have you ever wondered why some of your friends seem to lead more 'exciting' lives than yours? They seem to get the lucky breaks and their lives appear to have a lot more 'zing' than yours. If you are living your life along the lines of an NLE you are more likely to be letting things happen: your life is 'reactive'. Something happens to you, rather than you happening to something. By having a framework for your life, determining its direction and creating priorities, things can happen. Your life will become increasingly 'pro-active'. You call the shots in more situations, just like Annette.

Annette works in a local bank as a teller. She likes the routine and security that the bank appears to offer and she likes the people. But something is missing: she doesn't know what. Gerry works as a dress designer with a fashion house. He recently gave up a job he had with an insurance company (that paid more) but took a chance on this position after finishing an evening course. He decided that his future lay in fashion rather than life insurance. Gerry calls it his 'passion for fashion'. In a few weeks' time, he is going to Paris for a four-week study program on fashion and dressmaking techniques, paid for by his company. Although his future looks bright, he can't really predict what will await him six months, or even a year from now. Gerry finds that level of unpredictability very appealing. He's good at his work and doesn't crave 'job security'. His skills will travel with him. Annette, on the other hand, realises that a year, or even ten years, from now she'll probably be with the same bank, unless, of course, she is made redundant, a prospect she doesn't even want to think about.

If they were to meet, Annette would probably think that Gerry is 'lucky' but also quite reckless in his career choice; yet she would have a degree of envy. Gerry would regard Annette as too 'security conscious' and as someone who lacks an adventurous spirit or motivation to run her own life according to her own 'script'.

> Not everybody can be an explorer or an adventurer, but in your own small way you can take a step or two in that direction.

Not everybody can be an explorer or an adventurer, but in your own small way you can take a step or two in that direction. Your decision to make things happen can open all sorts of doors and contribute to living your life to the full.

Most of us probably know, or have heard of, people who have been diagnosed as being terminally ill, or others who, sadly, have died very young because of some illness or accident. Our reaction is generally to say 'Gee, you realise just how fragile and precious life is ... it's important to make the most of it, isn't it?' We say that, but do we really mean it? Are we prepared to make a commitment to it? Do we make the changes we fantasise or dream about? Very rarely. A day or two later, we are worrying about the dent on the car, or a date not working out last Saturday night. We quickly forget that moment of harsh reality when we are confronted by our own mortality and see things from another perspective. It's for precisely that reason that 'making it happen' is so important. It's part of not wanting to look back on your life and see it as a catalogue of missed opportunities, wasted time and regrets.

Begin to revel in the excitement that change brings, rather than fear it. It's all part of living your life to the full and squeezing everything you can out of every moment.

65
The fear of failure

Fear holds us back. It's real; we can feel the tension. When we get nervous about starting a new job, when we want just to make a change in our lives, we often simply get scared.

This fear prevents us from reaching our true potential. The fear is about being scared of failure. Just like some people say that they have a fear of flying, when what they really mean is that they have a fear of crashing. Our terminology masks the true meaning. We are not 'anxious' about our new job, we are scared of failing in it. We fear someone saying 'no' to us, so rather than risk a rejection, we just don't ask.

Often we also live up or down to people's expectations. Our failure (or success) can confirm other people's expectations of us: it becomes a self-fulfilling prophecy. If we can recognise, understand and then accept that fear is tying us down, we can begin to move forward from that point, and gradually overcome the fear. Sure, we are scared to take risks, worried about trying something new, but it's only by doing this that we grow and improve ourselves. As the saying goes, 'Calm seas never made a good sailor.' We need to be able to push ourselves, test ourselves, and poke and prod ourselves forward.

Sure, we might fail, but then we can learn from failure. Don't fall into the trap of taking it personally. Don't brand yourself a failure; forget the labels: YOU didn't fail. The idea may have failed, but you must keep trying. Why keep perpetuating your current situation? If you don't go out on a limb occasionally, how will you see the view? Sometimes you need to take it step by step; at other times you need to make a bolder move.

> If you don't go out on a limb occasionally, how will you see the view?

Either way, it's better than standing still. Your comfort zone will not only trap you, it may eventually suffocate you. If you treat mistakes as something you can learn from, you stop fearing failure. The sooner you fail (if, in fact, you do), the sooner you learn and move forward.

Failure is all about learning. It's falling off a bike then getting back on again. It's playing the wrong notes in music class. It's saying the wrong thing at the wrong time. Our own perception of failure colours it. It becomes a terrible thing. Treat failing as part of a learning experience, and then you'll grow. It's part of your journey. Every jolt and shock along the way improves and hones you. Steel needs fire and heat to temper and strengthen it ... so do you.

There is nothing that justifies a label that says 'failure'. Poor academic results don't; poor career choices don't; relationships that didn't work out don't. You are only a failure if you learn nothing from these experiences. Unfortunately, our society doesn't view failure as positive: we are led to believe that either you succeed or you don't. You hear people talking about a 'steep learning curve' when they are learning a new skill or a new job. It's another way of saying, 'I've got a lot to learn, and I'm sure I'll make mistakes, but that's okay because it's all a learning experience ... ' We don't say to people: 'It doesn't matter if you fail at this task: you'll know how to do it better next time ... ' Maybe we should.

The Fear of Failure

By not encouraging failure, we are not encouraging success either. It's like the songwriter who wrote forty songs before having a hit; an author who publishes fifteen novels before writing a best-seller. Each so-called failure added extra knowledge and insight, which led them closer to success.

History is littered with people who went the 'wrong' way or did the 'wrong' things, who learnt from their experience and went on to achieve great things without ever looking back. We spoke in chapter 27 about Christopher Columbus and Thomas Edison. Edison was labelled a 'no-hoper' at school. Albert Einstein was just an average student. Imagine a rock group which was initially rejected by a number of record companies: was the group a failure? The name of the group was The Beatles. Despite the obstacles and the rejections, they all pressed forward: their passion and belief in what they were doing carried them through. Learn the lessons of your 'failure': push past it and then leave it behind.

To all those who have ever failed: Congratulations.

66
Stress

Stress. Too little can be as bad as too much. We call stress an event or occurrence that you react to, that moves you to action. Thoughts and feelings can cause tension within you. In other words, stress is your reaction to an event of some description, real or imaginary. It could be an exam. It could be the thought of handing in a report the following morning. It could be how you feel prior to a job interview, or simply feeling overworked and crowded.

Being individuals, we all have differing reactions to stress. Some of us, for a whole variety of reasons, have better coping skills than others. An event that can devastate one person may be only a temporary inconvenience for another. Some people even relish and thrive in stressful situations while others fear the slightest variation in their daily routine.

> Coping with stress involves doing something positive ... What can you do right now to alleviate the stress?

It's important to acknowledge stress when we sense it, and examine our mood at the time. We may simply be over-reacting to something. Coping with stress involves doing something positive about the situation. It means that you are not like a creature immobilised by a beam of light, frozen, unable to move ... 'stressed out'. You need to understand the nature of your reaction. Analyse it. Calm down. What is it about the situation that is stressful? What can you do right now to alleviate the stress? Are you exaggerating the situation? This final point is an important one because we sometimes over-react to events without having all the facts to hand. For example, we may get stressed out because we believe that our boss is going to ask us about a report that we are working on. We get nervous and agitated, and guess what? It doesn't happen, the meeting is put off for a week. We were worried out of our minds for nothing. Yet we reacted as if it really had happened. We need to introduce some 'space' into the situation, and calmly think about the problem.

We are told that the mind cannot differentiate between a real and an imagined crisis. This means that when we think of some impending or even imaginary crisis, we experience all the nervous symptoms of stomach cramps, sweating, headaches, nail-biting and tension. These are all traits associated with a real event, yet they are not based on any real information; it's imagined. We need to develop the ability to react only to facts; that means delaying the response until all the information is to hand. Don't let an imagination working over-time drive you into panic.

There's an old saying that goes 'We'll cross that bridge when we come to it … ' Think about it. Many of us attempt to cross our bridges long before we even see them.

Take Cheryl, for example. She heard a rumour that the organisation she worked for was being taken over. The rumour spread like wildfire. Cheryl was convinced that her department was going to be closed down. She imagined all sorts of things going wrong, apart from losing her job. After a week of torture, the truth finally surfaced. Cheryl's organisation was, in fact, taking over another company. Her department was to be expanded. All that fear for nothing. She did not react to a fact, she reacted to an imaginary scenario created in her own mind. Had she waited for the facts, it would have been a different story. Cheryl crossed that bridge too early.

Many upheavals in life can cause stress, especially the unpredictable ones. These include changing or losing a job, a death in the family, shifting house and divorce or separation. We all cope differently with these events. Many things that happen are inevitable; we have no power over them. We need to learn which things can and cannot be changed.

Some people say 'It's not what you eat, but what's eating you'. Stress can 'eat you up' in a way. There are strong links between stress and disease. We've all heard of stressed-out executives dropping dead of a heart attack. Stress can cause a lot of physical and emotional damage. Here are a few simple things that you can do to help cope with the stress factors in your life.

1. Get some exercise. It helps put things back into perspective. Go for a walk, go jogging, ride a bike: just do something to divert your energies from your stress-inducing thoughts.
2. Stop, think, analyse. Is it really a problem? Can you deal with it straightaway? If you can, do so. If you can't, when can you deal with it? If you can't deal with it until next week, forget about it until then.
3. React only to facts. If it's not a fact don't react, because it could be a waste of time.
4. What's the worst that could happen? How terrible is it? Can you live with that consequence? If you can, get on with your life. If you can't, get some professional help, or seek advice from someone.
5. Take consolation from the fact that the majority of our fears and worries never happen. So many of them are simply products of an over-active mind.

6. Don't take your problems to bed with you. If you can't sleep, don't stay there tossing and turning or staring at the ceiling. Get up and read or do something else until you feel tired, then go back to bed. Bed is for sleeping, not worrying.

Keep the amount of stress in your life balanced. As we said earlier, too little is as bad as too much. Stress can be used wisely as a catalyst to propel you forward towards a better life or it can stop you completely. The choice is yours.

67
Developing a higher purpose
a view from the top

Have you ever been hot air ballooning? As you cruise high in the sky you can look down on things from a distance, and gain a broader perspective. The experience can be exhilarating. Taking a new perspective on your own life can also be exhilarating.

It's very easy to get caught up in the day-to-day stuff of life—work, study, family, friends, finances. All these things consume our energies, to the point where we have nothing in reserve. We need to actively participate in creating our own lives, our futures. This means taking responsibility for developing a higher purpose. We have to start by feeling that our lives matter to us (and to others) in a way that transcends the day-to-day routine. Even if the higher purpose we establish for ourselves is not a lofty one, it will allow us to improve on, and not simply become a prisoner of, the day-to-day routine.

> Taking a new perspective on your own life can also be exhilarating.

DEVELOPING A HIGHER PURPOSE

Why do we need to develop a higher view, a different perspective? To provide purpose and meaning to our lives, and to find a catalyst for our growth and development. A higher purpose, whether it is about effecting positive change in an organisation, community work, further study with a view to changing careers, or looking at ways we can help others, can be extremely enriching. It can help develop a great many aspects of ourselves, particularly our intellectual, emotional and spiritual selves, in a way that a total preoccupation with daily trivia can seldom achieve.

> It's a little like peeling an onion. We need to strip away layers of superficiality, and reveal an inner core of strength and harmony.

The development of a higher purpose is also likely to allow us to gain a more acute sense of who we are, what drives us, and what matters, in a way that is tremendously valuable. It can create a far deeper and more thoughtful response to the outer world. It's a little like peeling an onion. We need to strip away layers of superficiality, and reveal an inner core of strength and harmony. Each layer we peel away takes us a little closer to understanding and developing our higher purpose. This will allow us to remain focused on the priorities in our lives, while at the same time deal with, but not be overcome by, daily routines.

Whether or not we are conscious of it, we all have a need (and usually a desire) to better ourselves, to define ourselves and find some meaning and purpose in our lives. We might even say that this is the very essence of the human struggle, though that might be to miss the point. One of the real issues in this book is how to recognise our individual needs and deal with our own struggles in a way that defines

DEVELOPING A HIGHER PURPOSE

our higher purpose. This is hard work, like climbing a mountain. Step by step you progress and gradually reach the top. Once at the summit you look out at the view and see how magnificent it is. You tend to forget how difficult the journey was; you savour the moment. But then it's time to move on again, because the journey is never complete.

Once you have seen the view from the top of the mountain, it will be easier to understand the nature of your higher purpose. Part of it may be to make a wider contribution to the world: this in turn will give you the feeling that your life does matter and will help you when you start to waver or lose sight of your goals.

Developing a higher purpose is seldom easy, requiring as it does passion, commitment, energy and time. We eventually develop an ability to sift through the detail and devote ourselves to issues we consider important. We learn how to direct our time and energy into something that will allow us not only to look back on our life with a sense of purpose, but also to look forward and enjoy the journey. After all, we only get a one-way ticket.

68
Empowering others
what it's all about

Bookshops and libraries are filled with self-help books, many of which take a selfish perspective. They're all about 'me, me, me' and tend to ignore crucial aspects of life, such as how to deal and work with others, including family and friends. If you've read a self-help book, and you feel bolstered up and inspired, but your perspective is still selfish, then the book has in many ways failed. Your interpersonal skills are as important as your intrapersonal skills and the fashionable term for them is empowerment. Unfortunately, because this term is getting to be somewhat over-used it's essential to get behind the jargon, and remember what empowerment can do.

> Empowerment is a leadership skill. It allows you to bring out the best in other people.

Empowerment in a real sense is a leadership skill. It allows you to bring out the best in other people. It allows you to encourage initiative in others, and be able to step back, while someone else takes the credit for something. This can apply to friends, family, anybody you come into

Empowering others

contact with. It's about allowing others to reach their full potential, freeing yourself of any feelings of animosity or envy, and deriving satisfaction from seeing others do well.

Empowering others can take the form of actively encouraging others in their tasks, where your guidance and experience shows them the way without actually doing the job for them. This is where you take what you have learnt and direct it outwards so others can benefit from your knowledge. Empowerment is also about creating a caring, nurturing environment where people feel they have the support and encouragement to do their best and where they are not afraid to make a mistake but are helped to do things better and develop their talents to the full.

Kate, a talented graphic designer, was struggling with a fairly complex design for a logo that she couldn't get quite right. She decided to have a chat with Fiona, the creative director. The conversation was strange because Fiona didn't seem to offer her any direct advice or solution. Fiona simply asked Kate a few questions about her design and what the client was looking for, and other seemingly inconsequential questions. After about twenty minutes of this exchange, Kate left, a little confused by the whole encounter. She sat down at her desk. Suddenly she realised; Fiona was actually guiding her thinking, and focusing her approach to the task. Fiona didn't say this is how to do it, or how not to do the design, she simply made sure Kate was heading in the right direction. She was empowering Kate to keep going and to solve the problem. When Kate presented the idea to the client later that week he loved it, and Fiona was at the back of the room with a huge smile on her face. Fiona didn't need or want any credit. She saw her job as providing an environment of support and guidance in which others could do and be their best. The beauty of this approach is in the way Kate learnt from Fiona how to work with and guide others. As a consequence she will take an empowering approach herself as her career progresses.

You may feel sometimes that giving somebody a solution to a problem they're grappling with, or giving them a quick-fix answer, is helping them. It might not be. There's a saying: 'Give someone a fish and you feed them for a day; teach them to how to fish and you feed them for a lifetime.' That's what empowerment is all about.

Ironically, many managers in organisations believe that empowerment means telling people what to do. Such managers prefer to have people work for them, rather than with them.

Empowerment is as much about not doing as doing. Many have been empowered by teachers, gurus, mentors, friends and so on, not so much by their deeds but because of who they were, what they stood for, and for their inner strength. Your beliefs, values and ideas can be a source of inspiration to others. Don't underestimate your ability to empower others. People can look to you for advice or guidance. Your leadership can then be crucial. By living your own life with a sense of purpose and authenticity you may well empower others with your vision. By leading them to self-knowledge and awareness you empower others to do their best.

Ironically, there may be one selfish element to all of this. There is possibly no greater or more enriching feeling than guiding, inspiring and empowering others.

Part 8

Insight out

69
The best things in life are free

Yes, it's true, the best things in life are free, and the sooner we can stop and appreciate them, the richer our lives are likely to become.

Part of appreciating the abundance of beauty and vitality around you is relishing the fact that you can enjoy them. If you are sick in hospital, or are too ill to leave home, or just lack the capacity to appreciate the things around you, then it's difficult to take in and enjoy the sunsets, the mountains, fresh air, blossom on a tree, and other glorious things we commonly take for granted. The fact that you can value these things should in itself be appreciated.

In our headlong rush through a working week, and hectic social calendar, we often don't even notice the things closest to us. Next time you happen to be walking along a beach, stop for a moment and look around you. What can you see? What can you hear? Can you see the flutter of a sail on a yacht heading towards the horizon? Pick up a shell, look at its intricate

> Each day we should look upon the world as if we were seeing it for the first time.

design. Pick up a water-smoothed stone and think how many thousands, if not millions, of years old it could be. We need to re-educate ourselves and sometimes take a child's perspective on the world around us. Each day we should look upon the world as if we were seeing it for the first time.

As the seasons endlessly parade by your window, instead of moaning about the cold in winter, or the heat in summer, enjoy the seasons and what they bring. Accept the seasons and the changes as normal, and watch the bare trees blossom in spring, in readiness for the summer. By being more aware of the world around us, we can participate in it more, we can move out of ourselves, and begin to feel 'connected' to Nature.

In ancient times people were more attuned to the seasons, the stars, the ebb and flow of the tides. Rituals and customs were linked to the elements and the environment. We seem to have lost the capacity to feel a part of the planet we live on. So often we feel the need to harness and control Nature, instead of observing, learning and understanding it. Global warming, holes in the ozone layer, pollution ... these are all symptoms of humanity ignoring Nature and not heeding the warning signs. The world has become dominated by the economics of growth and development, at the cost of everything else.

> **The best things in life are ... things that money can't buy, things we remember forever.**

The best things in life are also more than just the beauty of the world we live in; they also reside in the people that we know. It is the birthday party of an old friend, it is the birth of a child, it is a smile of gratitude when we least expect it. Things that money can't buy are often things we remember forever.

We need to re-educate ourselves to realise that money isn't the key to happiness and contentment. There are so many things that we can appreciate and they don't cost a cent. We regularly need to get away from the chaos of city life and enjoy simple pleasures. If you can't get away, even doing something as simple as staring up at a starry sky at night can be a wondrous experience.

The best things in life *are* free. These are things that give meaning and substance to our lives, and prove to us that we are not robots, but feeling, caring humans who should never cease to wonder at the world we live in.

70
Stop and smell the roses

Time out. What's the rush? What is so important that we can't stop for just a moment? Remember when you were younger you could sit in the garden and seem to do nothing? To the 'untrained' eye you were doing nothing, but as far as you were concerned you were watching an ant struggling up the side of a blade of grass. You were watching a bee collect nectar from a flower, or you were simply looking around, and taking in the landscape of what seemed to be your enormous backyard or garden.

If an adult were to behave like this, we would be tempted to think that they were either a little crazy, lazy or both. We have learnt to feel guilty about just watching the sky, or seeing what happens when a leaf floats along a gutter ... and imagining what it would be like if we were sitting on that leaf ... what an adventure!

We are often so occupied watching TV, reading magazines, playing computer games, working, studying, eating, sleeping, that we rarely stop to smell the roses. Walk,

> ✻
> Put a STOP sign up and say that you've had enough. Get back in touch with yourself and your family.

Stop and Smell the Roses

run, ride, breathe it all in, enjoy it all. Regardless of whether you are a student, unemployed or a high-powered achiever, it's essential to take time out to enjoy the things around you.

If you have children, spend time with them, don't avoid them. Come home from your work as early as you can and just talk. Get to know each other. Just getting through each week can be a chore for many people, but taking some time out and getting to know your family better can help you regain some of that balance. Put a STOP sign up and say that you've had enough. Go for a drive, have a picnic, go to an amusement park. Get back in touch with yourself and your family.

It's true that many working parents are strangers to their children. Get your head out of work mode and into family mode. You may be a big success at work, but at home you are a father or mother, and a husband, wife or partner. You no longer have a job description. Besides, at home it doesn't count anyway. When you come home from work, what your child or partner has to say is important. Listen to each other. Thoughts about work can generally wait for an hour, or the whole evening ... can't they?

If you don't have the capacity to stop and smell the roses, to enjoy the things around you, to take time out, you are shutting out a vital part of your life and well-being. Life is about doing and not doing ... and knowing and appreciating the difference.

71
Is everything okay?

Now that you have read this far, we feel you should have a quick check to see that everything is okay. You may have given a lot of thought to some of the things we have written about. Some of it may have been challenging or even confronting, but we hope it has moved you to initiate some meaningful change in your life.

Asking yourself if everything is okay is also something that you can do quite regularly. It's almost like mentally taking a blood pressure test. It's not a bad idea to get in touch with yourself about how you feel right now. If things are going well, tap into yourself and see how you feel about it. If there is a crisis or some stress in your life, again see how you feel. Getting back in touch with yourself is an important tool in self-management. If we have a car we regularly check the oil and water, if we have a swimming pool we regularly check the water quality. Yet few people bother to do a simple maintenance check on themselves. While physical check-ups are important, so is the ability to see if everything is okay with the inner self.

> ✷
> Get in touch with yourself about how you feel right now.

Is everything okay?

Try not to fool yourself either. If things are not okay, acknowledge that, and move forward from that point. Hiding your head in the sand is the worst thing you can do. Face up to not being okay, and confront the problem, try to resolve it. If things are okay, then fine. If you find that all is not as it should be, then with some of the skills we have discussed, you should be able to make some progress. Do you need a break? Is the stress level at work too much? Is something troubling you at school? With a little self-knowledge you can begin to sort things out, or talk to someone else who can help. Above all, you can often heal yourself when things go wrong. It all starts with asking if you're okay. Okay?

72
Your life as an adventure

Whether we recognise or understand it now, our lives are a journey; a journey of discovery. How we choose to view them, and the type of adventures we participate in, are very much up to us. Our adventures can be short- or long-term, engaging or superficial, simple or difficult. We can participate fully or opt out simply by being spectators.

> ✮
> If you wait for the day when all is revealed . . . you may be waiting a long, long time.

Have you ever met anybody who seemed to be a spectator of their own lives in the sense that the world just passed them by? They seemed confused and felt that they couldn't do anything, however small, about their predicament. Even though they felt empty on the inside, they were seemingly helpless to change themselves in any meaningful way.

The journey we take is concerned with discovering more not only about ourselves but also about the world in which we exist, relate and communicate. There is little point in discovering things about ourselves in some vacuum—it is important to be able to channel the fruits of our discoveries in some positive direction, one that reinforces the sense of integration between the inner and outer worlds.

Our journey is also about stopping to observe and reflect on events and then moving on. It is about off-loading some old baggage, and taking on board some new lighter luggage in the form of new insights. It is about developing a central core of attitudes, values, beliefs and understanding the role that these play in motivating us to seek more insight along the way.

Our journey is a process in which we need to be constantly engaged—it is not about reaching a single destination. You have to get on and live your life as it is happening and not wait for some magical signal. After a while you are likely to realise that changes happen gradually over a considerable period of time. If you wait for the day when all is revealed to you about yourself you may be waiting a long, long time. You have to develop the ability to deal with all the issues that confront you along the way as part

> Time is the one ingredient we all have, although we never know how much.

of the journey. You have only one journey of discovery, one ride, and you have to seize the opportunity. You also have to try to integrate the inner and the outer journeys. There must be a sense of balance between the two; one without the other is likely to be empty.

Ultimately, life is to be seized and not put on hold. If we view life as a chore, something to be got through, we are in real trouble. Material possessions of all sorts come and go; the time we have simply goes. We probably all know people who have regrets, those who would like to have done this or that, if only they had the time. Time is the one ingredient we all have, although we never know how much. It is what we

Your life as an adventure

do with our time that is critical. Knowing that it is finite should propel us into action. We want to maximise our efforts to discover as much as we can for as long as we can.

Think back to past events in your life, some of the danger, some of the awkward moments, some of the pleasure and the pain. Looking back, does it look like an adventure? It's like watching a movie with you in the leading role. Well, why can't looking forward be an adventure as well?

Throughout our lives we can create opportunities and discover new adventures. We are free to choose which direction we will take. It's your life, so make it the adventure of a lifetime. There is no time like the present. Why not begin the real journey now?

73
Being present
enjoy the 'now'

Have you ever tried to put off your happiness or contentment? Have you ever said 'I'll be happy when I buy the new car' or 'I'll be happy when my holidays start' or 'I'll be happy when my promotion comes through'? It's all wrong. Many people's lives are filled with fear and loathing, as though they are waiting for some external event to make them happy such as a lottery win, an annual holiday, or perhaps some new purchase. Knowing how to enjoy the present is real happiness, but it isn't always as easy as it sounds.

> You can really only be useful to yourself and others in the PRESENT moment.

Many people have feelings of guilt and resentment about the past. They may also fear the future. With all this tension, their present moment is being destroyed because not only are they living in the past, but they also fear the future.

You live in the present moment. The moment you started reading this page is already in the past, it's gone, it's history. The future is yet to come, you haven't reached it yet. If you don't try to enjoy and maximise the NOW, the present moment in which you can effect change, then your future is going to be affected. You can really only be useful to yourself and others in the PRESENT moment. How often have you dreaded going to a meeting or an interview? You were full of fear and apprehension. You put all that energy into that FUTURE moment instead of ensuring that you get your act together NOW. If you act NOW in the PRESENT you may still be a little anxious about the meeting, but you may be better prepared for it.

Imagine Jake's bank manager calls him. It's annual review time, and the manager would like to discuss Jake's account. Jake is numb with fear, he doesn't sleep at night, he wakes at three in the morning in a cold sweat, he has nightmares of the manager tearing up his bank statements and throwing him out of the bank, laughing madly as Jake hits the footpath. Jake is too future oriented for his own good.

Alice also received a letter from her bank manager. She went to her accountant who prepared some documents including cash flow projections and a balance sheet. She slept well because she took care of the PRESENT without being immobilised by an imaginary fear of the future. Oh, and what happened to Jake? The meeting was cancelled; fortunately, he has two more weeks to organise himself.

What about the person who always thinks things will be different or better tomorrow, but does nothing about it? Tomorrow never comes. Or the person who puts their life on hold waiting for the weekend. By living effectively in the PRESENT you can create your own FUTURE. Nothing will happen tomorrow if you don't act today. Today is the opportunity you have to make a difference in your life, so don't waste it.

We cannot escape the past, because it has shaped what we are today. We have to deal with our past, resolve all the regrets, conflicts, fears and guilt and move into the light that

Being present

represents an excellent 'today' and an even better 'tomorrow'. Only by owning and integrating our past into the present can we grow and move forward in a way that gives us a chance to achieve our dreams. We must refuse to embrace mediocrity, something that's just 'okay'. We all deserve more. Again, this links into whether we make things happen, or let things happen. How we act today will make a difference tomorrow; it will also help determine whether our mission statement helps to create a future or binds us to our past.

We can only react to and be effective in the present moment. We can only react to NOW. We can't react in advance. It's all a matter of your thinking matching your circumstances. React to NOW by living in the present moment. Sure, be future-oriented, pay your bills, keep your dental appointments and so on, but live, enjoy and be effective in the NOW.

These really are the 'good old days'. What you are living through now will be the nostalgia of next week. Can you remember what was worrying you a year ago, or even a month ago? Probably not: your life has moved forward.

>   Birth is a beginning
>   And death a destination.
>   And life is a journey:
>   From childhood to maturity
>   And youth to age;
>   From innocence to awareness
>   And ignorance to knowing;
>   From foolishness to discretion
>   And then, perhaps to wisdom;
>   From weakness to strength
>   Or strength to weakness—

And, often, back again;
From health to sickness
And back, we pray, to health again;
From offense to forgiveness,
From loneliness to love,
From joy to gratitude,
From pain to compassion,
And grief to understanding—
   From fear to faith;
From defeat to defeat to defeat—
Until, looking backward or ahead,
We see that victory lies
Not at some high place along the way,
But in having made the journey, stage by stage,
   A sacred pilgrimage.
Birth is a beginning
And death a destination.
And life is a journey,
A sacred pilgrimage—
   To life everlasting.

Central Conference of American Rabbis: 'Birth is a Beginning', by Alvin I. Fine. From *Gates of Repentance*, edited by Chaim Stern. Copyright © 1978. Reprinted by permission of the CCAR.

Further reading

Beck, Charlotte Joko. *Nothing Special: Living Zen*, HarperSanFrancisco, 1993.
Buscaglia, Leo F. *Personhood*, Ballantine Books, 1978.
Capra, Fritjof. *Uncommon Wisdom*, Fontana Paperbacks, 1988.
Cusick, Anne. *Choices*, Simon & Schuster, 1990.
Deng, Ming-Dao. *Scholar Warrior An Introduction to the Tao in Everyday Life*, HarperSanFrancisco, 1990.
Dowrick, Stephanie. *Intimacy and Solitude*, William Heinemann, 1991.
Dossey, Larry. *Healing Breakthroughs*, Piatkus Publishing, 1991.
Dreher, Diane. *The Tao of Inner Peace*, HarperCollins, 1990.
Dyer, Wayne W. *Pulling Your Own Strings*, Hamlyn Paperbacks, 1978.
Fromm, Erich. *To Have or to Be?*, Abacus, 1979.
Gawain, Shakti. *Living in the Light*, Whatever Publishing Inc., 1986.
Harris, Philip. *The Spiritual Path to Complete Fulfilment*, Hill of Content, 1993.
Hill, Napoleon. *Think and Grow Rich*, (new edition) Wilshire Book Company.
Hopson, Barrie & Scally, Mike. *Build Your Own Rainbow*, Mercury Books, 1991.
Jamplosky, Gerald. *Love is Letting Go of Fear*, Celestial Arts, 1979.
Johnson, Robert. *Inner Work*, Harper & Row, 1989.
Johnson, Robert. *Owning Your Own Shadow*, HarperCollins, 1991.
Johnson, Robert. *Transformation*, HarperCollins, 1991.

Further Reading

Kowalski, Reinhard. *Discovering Your Self*, Routledge, 1993.
Krishnamurti. *Meeting Life*, Arkana, 1991.
Macnab, Francis. *Footprints*, Hyland House, 1994.
Maltz, Maxwell. *Psycho-Cybernetics*, Pocket Books, 1969.
Mitchell, Stephen. *Tao Te Ching*, Harper & Row, 1988.
Moore, Tony. *Cry of the Damaged Man*, Picador, 1991.
Ouspensky, P. D. *The Psychology of Man's Possible Evolution*, Vintage, 1974.
O'Connor, Joseph & Seymour, John. *Introducing NLP Neuro Linguistic Programming*, Aquarian–Thorsons, 1990.
Orbach, Susie. *What's Really Going On?*, Virago Press, 1994.
Samways, Louise. *Dangerous Persuaders*, Penguin, 1994.
Solomon, Robert C. *The Passions*, Hackett Publishing Co., 1993.
Smedes, Lewis B. *A Pretty Good Person*, HarperCollins, 1991.
Tysoe, Maryon. *Love Isn't Quite Enough*, HarperCollins–Fontana, 1992.
Wilhelm, Richard. *Lectures on the I Ching*, Routledge and Kegan Paul, 1980.
Zohar, Danah. *The Quantum Self*, HarperCollins–Flamingo, 1990.